Knitting

in the Details

CHARMING DESIGNS TO KNIT & EMBELLISH

Louisa Harding

INTERWEAVE
interweave.com

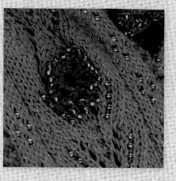

EDITOR Ann Budd
TECHNICAL EDITOR Kristen TenDyke
PHOTOGRAPHER Stephen Jessup
ART DIRECTOR Liz Quan
COVER AND INTERIOR DESIGN Karla Baker
PRODUCTION Katherine Jackson

Interweave Press LLC
201 East Fourth Street
Loveland, CO 80537-5655 USA
interweave.com

Printed in China by Asia Pacific Offset, Ltd.

Library of Congress Cataloging-in-Publication Data

Harding, Louisa.
  Knitting in the details : charming designs to knit and embellish /
Louisa Harding.
     p. cm.
  Includes index.
  ISBN 978-1-59668-256-6 (pbk.)
  1. Knitting. 2. Knitting--Patterns. I. Title.
  TT820.H2658 2010
  746.43--dc22
        2010021177

10 9 8 7 6 5 4 3 2 1

ACKNOWLEDGMENTS

'To understand your parents' love
 bear your own children'

This book is for my mother, Daphne, a constant source of strength, support, and unconditional love.

As always I thank Stephen Jessup for wonderful photographs and for being my rock and our children, Belle and Oscar, thankfully, children change everything.

This book would not be possible without the help of the following people; my wonderful knitters, Betty Rothwell, Betty Marsh, Daphne Harding, Mary Butler, Mrs. Wilmot, Debbie Humphreys, and Jenny Carter.

I would like to thank the models, Joanna Stubbs, Aby Fox, and Sheri Staplehurst, as well as Liz Rochford for being such a wonderfully creative makeup and hair artist, and Guy Bishop, our photographer's assistant.

Finally, thank you to Tricia Waddell and Rebecca Campbell and the fantastic team of editors, book designers, and production people at Interweave for their support, understanding, and encouragement.

INTRODUCTION

In my studio, I have an evergrowing collection of boxes, tins, baskets, and jars that contain my many treasures. Instead of rubies and diamonds, my riches include such things as an unruly tangle of ribbons that grows like an overflowing porridge pot in a children's fairy tale.

My desire to collect all things that sparkle or glisten is insatiable. I love anything that looks as if it has a hidden story, such as a vintage brooch at the thrift shop, a jar of old belt buckles in the dusty corner of my local haberdashery shop, and my mother's jewelry boxes filled with broken trinkets. I am compelled to collect and surround myself with these castoffs, waiting for a flash of inspiration to give these once-loved items a continuing story.

Not all my treasures are found objects, however. Some are quite new. During a trip to Paris a few years ago, I visited La Droguerie—a store devoted to buttons, beads, ribbons, feathers, and all sorts of enticing gems. I spent hours picking out velvet ribbon, a frenzy of feathers, and beautifully handcrafted artisan buttons. This store fueled my lust for embellishments with every one of the thousands of items displayed with love in glass jars and on wooden reels. Haberdashery shops are not always easy to find, hidden away like little gems, but they are always staffed with wonderful people knowledgeable about thousands of products.

This book, *Knitting in the Details,* is the beginning of the story I want to tell about using beautiful embellishments for knitted projects. Knitting is a wonderfully creative pursuit that is both meditative and relaxing, and while there are many patterns and yarns for fantastic projects, I believe that a bit of personal history or added creativity enhances each piece. For me, embellishment is about adding buttons from an old shirt to the edging of a scarf or the charms from a broken bracelet to the flounce on a purse. It is about rediscovering techniques that my grandmother's generation used to add decoration to their work—embroidery, beading, and appliqué—all skills that make a project unique. In our world of availability and mass production, it is comforting to revisit these techniques to make appealing projects.

There is a Chinese proverb that says "Patience and the mulberry leaf make a silk purse." Many of the knitted projects in this book are simple and quick to knit. The love is in the embellishment—taking the time to add a special detail, a finishing touch, a unique quality. This love prolongs the story and the history of each piece to create heirlooms of the future. I hope that the projects contained in these pages will inspire you to add your personal history into your own unique projects.

embroidery

Embroidery is one of the most delightful methods of enhancing a knitted project. Amber (page 10), a cloche-style hat, has just a small amount of embroidery, whereas Opal (page 18), a striped purse, is heavily embellished with a combination of stitches. Lazy daisy embroidery and French knots add texture and color to Erin (page 14), a simple beret pattern. Ruby (page 22), a gift purse with ribbon ties knitted in two very different and contrasting yarns, is embellished with cross-stitches. Versatile duplicate stitch is used in very different ways in the Coral cardigan (page 26) and Flora pullover (page 34), illustrating a couple of ways to use this stitch.

FINISHED SIZE
About 20¼" (51.5 cm) head
circumference.

YARN
Worsted weight (#4 Medium).

SHOWN HERE: Louisa Harding Kashmir Aran (55% wool, 10% cashmere,
35% microfiber; 83 yd [76 m]/50 g).

Striped version: #39 Pansy (purple; A),
2 balls; #40 Cloud (light blue; B) and
#38 Blush (pink; C), 1 ball each.

Solid version: #12 Grey, 3 balls.

Louisa Harding Sari Ribbon (90% nylon, 10% metallic, 66 yd [60 m]/50 g):
#37 Twilight, small amounts for solid
version only.

NEEDLES
Sides and crown: size U.S. 7 (4.5 mm).

Brim: size U.S. 8 (5 mm).

*Adjust needle size if necessary to
obtain the correct gauge.*

NOTIONS
Tapestry needle; 31½" (80 cm) of
16-gauge silver-plated jewelry wire;
oddments of yarn for embroidery for
striped version.

GAUGE
18 stitches and 32 rows = 4" (10 cm)
in seed stitch with smaller needles.

Amber

To strengthen the brims of these cloche-style hats, I worked
them in a knitted woven-stitch pattern. To help them hold their
shape, I threaded jewelry wire through the cast-on stitches; you
can omit the wire if you prefer a floppy casual look. I embellished the band of the striped version (page 12) and the left
side of the solid version with lazy daisy stitches worked at different scales to create two completely different looks.

Solid version.

Striped Version

With A and larger needles, CO 121 sts. Knit 1 row.

Brim

INC ROW: (WS) K3, *M1 (see Glossary), k4; rep from * to last 2 sts, M1, k2—151 sts.

ROW 1: (RS) *K1, sl 1 pwise with yarn in front (wyf), bring yarn to back; rep from * to last st, k1.

ROW 2: Sl 1 pwise with yarn in back (wyb), bring yarn to front, *p1, sl 1 pwise wyb, bring yarn to front; rep from * to last 2 sts, k1, sl 1.

Rep these 2 rows 7 more times, then work Row 1 once again and at the same time work the foll color sequence: *4 rows A, 4 rows B, 2 rows A, 2 rows C, 2 rows A; rep from *—piece measures about 1¾" (4.5 cm) from CO.

DEC ROW: (WS) K1, *k2tog, k1, k2tog; rep from *—91 sts rem.

Sides

With B and smaller needles, work 2 rows in garter st (knit every row).

With A, knit 1 RS row, then work seed st as foll:

ROW 1: (WS) *K1, p1; rep from * to last st, k1.

ROW 2: (RS) *K1, p1; rep from * to last st, k1.

Rep these 2 rows 3 more times, then work Row 1 once more.

Change to B and work 2 rows in garter st. Change to A and knit 1 RS row. Work 3 rows even in seed st. Cont in seed st and at the same time work the foll color sequence: *1 row B, 1 row C, 2 rows A, 1 row C, 1 row B, 4 rows A; rep from * once.

Shape Crown

ROW 1: (RS) *P7, p2tog; rep from * to last st, p1—81 sts rem.

ROWS 2, 4, 6, 8, 10, 12, AND 14: Knit.

Striped version.

ROW 3: *P6, p2tog; rep from * to last st, p1—71 sts rem.

ROW 5: *P5, p2tog; rep from * to last st, p1—61 sts rem.

ROW 7: *P4, p2tog; rep from * to last st, p1—51 sts rem.

ROW 9: *P3, p2tog; rep from * to last st, p1—41 sts rem.

ROW 11: *P2, p2tog; rep from * to last st, p1—31 sts rem.

ROW 13: *P1, p2tog; rep from * to last st, p1—21 sts rem.

ROW 15: *P2tog; rep from * to last st, p1—11 sts rem.

ROW 16: Knit.

Cut yarn, leaving a 6" (15 cm) tail. Thread tail through rem sts, pull tight, and fasten off on WS.

Solid Version

With larger needles, CO 121 sts. Knit 1 row.

Brim

Work as for striped version, but omit color changes—91 sts rem.

Sides

Change to smaller needles and work 2 rows in garter st (knit every row). Work seed st as foll:

ROW 1: (WS) *K1, p1; rep from * to last st, k1.

ROW 2: (RS) *K1, p1; rep from * to last st, k1.

Rep these 2 rows 3 more times, then work Row 1 once more. Work 3 rows in garter st, ending with a RS row. Work 21 rows in seed st as foll: *k1, p1; rep from * to last st, k1.

Shape Crown

Shape Crown as for striped version.

Finishing

Weave in loose ends. Block to finished measurements.

Embellishment

Striped version: With B threaded on a tapestry needle and using the photograph as a guide, embroider 3-petal lazy daisies (see page 31) on the top and bottom of the seed-stitch brim. With A, embroider 4-petal lazy daisies across the center of the band.

Solid version: With ribbon yarn threaded on a tapestry needle and using the photograph as a guide, embroider different sizes of 5-petal lazy daisies (see page 31) on the left side of the hat.

Seam and Wire

With yarn (A for striped version) threaded on a tapestry needle, use a mattress st or backstitch (see Glossary) to sew sides tog. Starting at the seam, thread the jewelry wire through the CO sts at base of brim. Twist the two ends of wire around each other to secure. With yarn (A for striped version) threaded on a tapestry needle, use whipstitches (see Glossary) to secure the wire in place.

FINISHED SIZE

About 19½" (49.5 cm) in circumference. To fit an average-size female.

YARN

Worsted weight (#4 Medium).

SHOWN HERE: Louisa Harding Grace Silk and Wool (50% merino, 50% silk; 110 yd [101 m]/50 g): #23 Sloe (purple), 2 balls.

NEEDLES

Sides and crown: size U.S. 7 (4.5 mm).

Edging: size U.S. 4 (3.5 mm).

Adjust needle size if necessary to obtain the correct gauge.

NOTIONS

Tapestry needle; oddments of yarn for embroidery.

GAUGE

20 stitches and 28 rows = 4" (10 cm) in stockinette stitch on larger needles.

Erin

This chic beret features an elegant mock cable edging and embroidered lazy daisies. Worked before the seam is sewn, the embroidery is worked in layers, one daisy on top of another. The center of each daisy is finished with a contrasting French knot. Use a variety of yarns you have in your stash or embroidery threads to experiment with different color combinations and placements until you're satisfied with the look—be confident in your creativity.

Beret

With smaller needles, work picot CO as folls: *Use the cable method (see Glossary) to CO 5 sts, BO 2 sts, slip st from right needle tip onto left needle tip (2 sts on left needle tip); rep from * 32 times, use the cable method to CO 2 more sts—98 sts. Work in mock cable rib as folls:

ROW 1: (RS) K1, *p2, k2; rep from * to last st, k1.

ROW 2: K1, *p2, k2; rep from * to last st, k1.

ROW 3: K1, *p2, RC (see Stitch Guide); rep from * to last st, k1.

ROW 4: K1, *p2, k2; rep from * to last st, k1.

Rep these 4 rows 4 more times, ending with WS row.

INC ROW: (RS) K1, M1 (see Glossary), *k3, M1; rep from * to last 4 sts, k2, M1, k2—131 sts.

NEXT ROW: K1, purl to last st, k1.

Change to larger needles and, beg with a knit row, work 24 rows in St st (knit RS rows; purl WS rows).

DEC ROW 1: (RS) *K8, k2tog; rep from * to last st, k1—118 sts rem.

Work 7 rows even in St st.

DEC ROW 2: *K7, K2tog; rep from * to last st, k1—105 sts rem.

Work 3 rows even in St st.

DEC ROW 3: *K6, k2tog; rep from * to last st, k1—92 sts rem.

Work 3 rows even in St st.

DEC ROW 4: *K5, k2tog; rep from * to last st, k1—79 sts rem.

Work 3 rows even in St st.

DEC ROW 5: *K4, k2tog; rep from * to last st, k1—66 sts rem.

Work 1 WS row even.

DEC ROW 6: *K3, k2tog; rep from * to last st, k1—53 sts rem.

Work 1 WS row even.

DEC ROW 7: *K2, k2tog; rep from * to last st, k1—40 sts rem.

Work 1 WS row even.

DEC ROW 8: *K1, k2tog; rep from * to last st, k1—27 sts rem.

DEC ROW 9: (WS) P1, *p2tog; rep from *—14 sts rem.

Break yarn, thread tail through rem sts, pull tight to close hole, and secure on WS.

Finishing

Weave in loose ends. Block to finished measurements.

Embroidery

With oddments of yarn threaded on a tapestry needle, embroider lazy daisies with 5 petals (see page 31) randomly to beret front. With contrasting colors, work a French knot (see page 31) in the center of each daisy.

With yarn threaded on a tapestry needle, use a mattress st or backstitch (see Glossary) to sew seam.

FINISHED SIZE

About 11¼" (28.5 cm) wide and 13½" (34.5 cm) long, excluding edging.

YARN

Aran weight (#4 Medium).

SHOWN HERE: Harding Kashmir Aran (55% wool, 10% cashmere, 35% microfiber; 83 yd [76 m]/50 g): #38 Blush (A), 2 balls; #37 Pearl (off-white; B), #6 Grass Green (C), #36 Frost (gray-blue; D), and #42 Banana (yellow; E), 1 ball each.

NEEDLES

Sizes U.S. 7 and 8 (4.5 and 5 mm).

Adjust needle size if necessary to obtain the correct gauge.

NOTIONS

Stitch holder; tapestry needle; one pair of 11" (28 cm) round-top bag handles.

GAUGE

18 stitches and 24 rows = 4" (10 cm) in stockinette stitch on larger needles.

Opal

This simple striped purse makes great use of stash yarn. The knitted fabric provides a blank canvas for you to embellish to your heart's content. I have used the leftover yarns to work a combination of half and full lazy daisies, duplicate stitch, cross-stitch, chain stitch, and French knots. I have even added a chain-stitch flourish on each side of the heart. Choose whatever you have on hand to make the purse your own.

Back

With A and smaller needles, CO 51 sts. Beg with a RS row, work 10 rows in St st (knit RS rows; purl WS rows), ending with a WS row. Change to E and knit 2 rows (1 garter ridge on RS for fold line). Change to B and larger needles.

ROWS 1, 3, 5, 7, AND 9: (RS) Knit.

ROWS 2, 4, 6, AND 8: (WS) K3, p45, k3.

ROW 10: With E, k3, p45, k3.

ROWS 11–19: With A, work in patt as established.

ROW 20: With E, rep Row 10.

ROWS 21–29: With C, work in patt as established.

ROW 30: With E, rep Row 10.

Cont working all sts in St st and beg with a RS row, work 2 rows with B.

INC ROW: (RS) With B, k3, M1 (see Glossary), knit to last 3 sts, M1, k3—2 sts inc'd.

With B, work 6 rows even, ending with a RS row. With E, work 1 WS row. With D, work 2 rows, then rep inc row—55 sts. With D, work 6 rows even, ending with a RS row. With E, work 1 WS row. With A, work 2 rows, then rep inc row—57 sts. With A, work 6 rows even, ending with a RS row. With E, work 1 WS row. With C, work 2 rows, then rep inc row—59 sts. With C, work 6 rows even, ending with a RS row. With E, work 1 WS row. With D, work 9 rows even, ending with a RS row. With E, work 2 rows, ending with RS row—piece measures about 15½" (39.5 cm) from CO. Place sts on holder.

Front

CO and work as for bag back.

Finishing

Place bag back and front on separate needles. Hold needles with WS facing tog and, with E, use the three-needle method (see Glossary) to BO the sts tog, forming a ridge (fold line) on the outside of the bag.

Edging

With E and smaller needles, CO 7 sts.

With WS facing, knit 1 row. Rep Rows 1–4 of Edging chart until edging is same length as base of bag, ending with Row 4 of patt. BO all sts.

Block to finished measurements.

Embellishment

Using the embellishment diagram as a guide (see page 31 for embroidery instructions), work duplicate st, cross st, chain st, lazy daisy st (with 2, 3, 4, or 5 petals as indicated), and French knots on the bag front.

Assembly

With WS tog, fold bag in half at bottom fold-line. With E threaded on a tapestry needle, use a whipstitch (see Glossary) to sew the straight edge of the edging to fold line. With WS facing tog, use the mattress st (see Glossary) to sew front and back tog from fold line to start of garter-st edging. Rep for seam on other side.

Slip one CO edge through gap in handle. Whip-stitch CO edge to WS of bag, using fold line as a guide. Rep for other handle.

EDGING CHART

- ☐ knit on RS, purl on WS
- ● purl on RS, knit on WS
- ╱ k2tog
- ◯ yo
- ⌒ BO

EMBELLISHMENT DIAGRAM

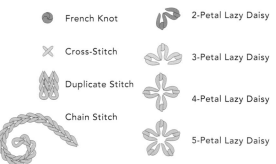

French Knot

Cross-Stitch

Duplicate Stitch

Chain Stitch

2-Petal Lazy Daisy

3-Petal Lazy Daisy

4-Petal Lazy Daisy

5-Petal Lazy Daisy

Mulberry silk purse: about 11½"
(29 cm) wide and 11" (28 cm) long.

Hulda purse: about 14¾" (37.5 cm)
wide and 17" (43 cm) long.

YARN
DK weight (#3 Light) or Chunky
weight (#5 Bulky).

SHOWN HERE: Louisa Harding
Mulberry Silk (100% silk; 136 yd
[124 m]/50 g): #6 Pink (A), 2 balls;
#4 Rose (B), 1 ball.

Louisa Harding Hulda (50% wool,
30% acrylic, 20% linen; 110 yd
[101 m]/50 g): #8 Charcoal (A),
3 balls; #12 Girly (B), 1 ball.

NEEDLES
Mulberry Silk version: sizes U.S. 3
and 6 (3.25 and 4 mm).

Hulda version: sizes U.S. 8 and 10
(5 and 6 mm).

*Adjust needle size if necessary to
obtain the correct gauge.*

NOTIONS
Stitch holders; tapestry needle;
about 62" (157.5 cm) of ⅝" (1.5 cm)
ribbon for Mullberry Silk purse;
about 79" (200 cm) of 1¼" (3.2 cm)
ribbon for Hulda purse.

GAUGE
Mulberry Silk version: 22 stitches
and 30 rows = 4" (10 cm) in stockinette stitch on larger needles.

Hulda version: 17 stitches and 21
rows = 4" (10 cm) in stockinette
stitch on larger needles.

Ruby

This purse requires just a few balls of yarn, is quick to knit, and
is just right for customizing. I have shown two versions, both
worked on the same number of stitches—one is worked in a
DK weight silk for glamour (page 24), and one is worked in a
bulky-weight wool-linen blend for a more rustic feel. The size of
the yarn determines the size of the purse. Both are embellished
with cross-stitch embroidery hearts.

Hulda version.

Note

Measurements are given for Mulberry Silk purse with Hulda purse in parentheses.

Back

With B and smaller needles, CO 63 sts. Work 2 rows in garter st (knit every row). Change to A and larger needles. Work Rows 1–8 of Lace chart, then work Rows 1–4 once more—piece measures about 2 (3)" (5 [7.5] cm) from CO. Work 2 rows in garter st. Change to B and work 3 rows in garter st.

EYELET ROW: (WS) K1, p1, *yo, p2tog; rep from * to last st, k1.

Work 2 rows in garter st. Change to A and work 2 rows in garter st. Beg with a RS row, work even in St st (knit RS rows; purl WS rows) until piece measures 11 (17)" (28 [43] cm) from CO, ending with a WS row. Place sts on holder.

Front

CO and work as for back.

Finishing

Weave in loose ends. Block to finished measurements. Place held back and front sts on needles, hold with WS tog, and use the three-needle method (see Glossary) to BO the sts tog.

Embroidery

With B threaded on a tapestry needle, work cross-stitch embroidery (see page 31) as shown at right.

Mulberry Silk version.

Assembly

With WS tog, fold bag in half along bottom foldline. With A threaded on a tapestry needle, use a mattress st (see Glossary) to sew side seams. Cut ribbon in half. Starting at opposite sides of bag, thread each length of ribbon through eyelets at bag top. Knot the ends.

CROSS-STITCH DIAGRAMS

Mulberry Silk   *Hulda*

LACE CHART

☐	knit on RS, purl on WS	◉ yo
◉	purl on RS, knit on WS	⋏ sl 1, k2tog, psso
╱	k2tog	☐ pattern repeat
╲	ssk	

FINISHED SIZE
About 32 (34, 35¾, 37½, 39¾, 41)"
(81.5 [86.5, 91, 95, 101, 104] cm)
bust circumference, with about 1"
to 2" (2.5 to 5 cm) of ease. Sweater
shown measures 32" (81.5 cm).

YARN
Worsted weight (#4 Medium).

SHOWN HERE: Louisa Harding
Thistle (60% merino, 40% suri
alpaca; 98 yd [90 m]/50 g): #8 Berry
(A), 2 (2, 3, 3, 4, 4) balls; #5 Old
Rose (B) and #2 Oatmeal (D), 3 (3,
3, 4, 4, 4) balls each; #3 Stone (C),
2 (2, 3, 3, 4, 4) balls.

NEEDLES
Body and sleeves: size U.S. 8
(5 mm): 32" (80 cm) circular (cir).

Edging: size U.S. 7 (4.5 mm): 32"
(80 cm) cir.

Adjust needle size if necessary to
obtain the correct gauge.

NOTIONS
Markers (m); stitch holders; tapestry needle.

GAUGE
18 stitches and 24 rows = 4"
(10 cm) in stockinette stitch on
larger needles.

Coral

This lovely sweater is detailed with duplicate stitch—also called
Swiss darning—to add color and pattern after the knitting is
complete. This versatile treatment gives the hem of this striped
cardigan the look of a complicated Fair Isle border. The tech-
nique takes a little practice, so you might want to begin with
the smaller pattern on the sleeves. Once mastered, it can be
used to introduce complicated-looking color and pattern to an
array of knitted projects.

Stitch Guide

Color Pattern (worked in St st)

ROWS 1 AND 2: Work center St sts with C.

ROW 3: Work center St sts with B.

ROWS 4–9: Work center St sts with D.

ROW 10: Work center St sts with B.

ROWS 11 AND 12: Work center St sts with C.

ROWS 13–16: Work center St sts with B.

Repeat Rows 1–16 for color pattern.

Notes

The body is worked in one piece to the armholes on circular needles to accommodate the large number of stitches.

The color pattern is worked in the intarsia method of using a separate ball or strand of yarn for each color area and twisting the yarns around each other at color changes.

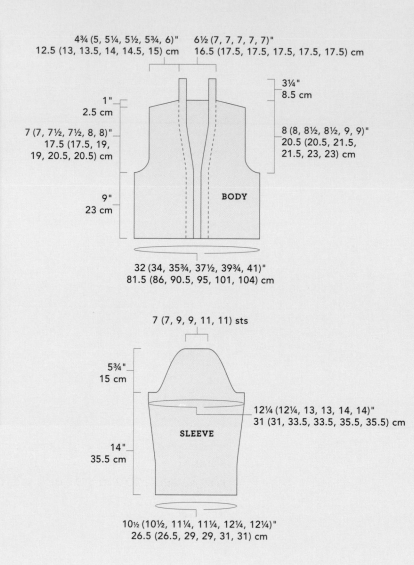

4¾ (5, 5¼, 5½, 5¾, 6)"
12.5 (13, 13.5, 14, 14.5, 15) cm

6½ (7, 7, 7, 7, 7)"
16.5 (17.5, 17.5, 17.5, 17.5, 17.5) cm

1"
2.5 cm

3¼"
8.5 cm

7 (7, 7½, 7½, 8, 8)"
17.5 (17.5, 19, 19, 20.5, 20.5) cm

8 (8, 8½, 8½, 9, 9)"
20.5 (20.5, 21.5, 21.5, 23, 23) cm

BODY

9"
23 cm

32 (34, 35¾, 37½, 39¾, 41)"
81.5 (86, 90.5, 95, 101, 104) cm

7 (7, 9, 9, 11, 11) sts

5¾"
15 cm

12¼ (12¼, 13, 13, 14, 14)"
31 (31, 33.5, 33.5, 35.5, 35.5) cm

SLEEVE

14"
35.5 cm

10½ (10½, 11¼, 11¼, 12¼, 12¼)"
26.5 (26.5, 29, 29, 31, 31) cm

Body

With A and smaller needle, work picot CO as foll: *Use the cable method (see Glossary) to CO 5 sts, BO 2 sts, slip st from right needle tip onto left needle tip (3 sts on left-hand needle); rep from * until there are 147 (153, 162, 171, 180, 186) sts, use the cable method to CO 0 (2, 1, 0, 1, 1) more st(s)—147 (155, 163, 171, 181, 187) sts. Do not join. Work 2 rows in garter st (knit every row), ending with a WS row.

Work striped garter st and edging patt as foll:

EDGING ROW 1: (RS) With A, k2, yo, k2tog, k4, place marker (pm), change to B, k131 (139, 147, 155, 165, 171), pm, join new ball of A and k5, yo, k2tog, k1.

EDGING ROW 2: With A, k2, yo, k2tog, k4, slip marker (sl m), with B, knit to m, sl m, with A, k5, yo, k2tog, k1.

EDGING ROWS 3 AND 4: With A, use the cable method to CO 2 sts, BO 2 sts (1 st on right needle tip), k1, yo, k2tog, k4, sl m, with C, knit to m, sl m, with A, k5, yo, k2tog, k1.

EDGING ROWS 5 AND 6: With A, k2, yo, k2tog, k4, sl m, with D, knit to m, sl m, with A, k5, yo, k2tog, k1.

EDGING ROWS 7 AND 8: With A, CO 2 sts, BO 2 sts (1 st on right needle tip), k1, yo, k2tog, k4, sl m, with B, knit to m, sl m, with A, k5, yo, k2tog, k1.

Change to larger needle and work St st color patt and edging patt as folls:

ROW 1: (RS) With A, k2, yo, k2tog, k4, sl m, knit to next m with appropriate color (see Stitch Guide), sl m, with A, k5, yo, k2tog, k1.

ROW 2: With A, k2, yo, k2tog, k4, sl m, purl to next m with appropriate color, sl m, with A, k5, yo, k2tog, k1.

ROW 3: With A, CO 2 sts, BO 2 sts (1 st on right needle tip), k1, yo, k2tog, k4, sl m, knit to next m with appropriate color, sl m, with A, k5, yo, k2tog, k1.

ROW 4: With A, CO 2 sts, BO 2 sts (1 st on right needle tip), k1, yo, k2tog, k4, sl m, purl to next m with appropriate color, sl m, with A, k5, yo, k2tog, k1.

Following the 16-row color patt, rep these 4 rows until piece measures 9" (23 cm) from CO, ending with a WS row. Make note of the last row of color patt worked.

Right Front

Note: The neck and armhole are shaped at the same time.

With A and RS facing, work in patt to m, sl m, use appropriate color to ssk, k27 (29, 31, 33, 35, 37) sts, turn—36 (38, 40, 42, 44, 46) sts rem for right front; rem 110 (116, 122, 128, 136, 140) sts will be worked later for back and left front. Work right front sts back and forth in rows as foll:

DEC ROW 1: (WS) Keeping in patt, BO 4 (4, 5, 6, 6, 6) sts, purl to m, sl m, with A, work to end in patt—32 (34, 35, 36, 38, 40) sts rem.

DEC ROW 2: (RS) Keeping in patt, work to m, sl m, use appropriate color to ssk (neck dec), knit to last 2 sts, k2tog (armhole dec)—2 sts dec'd.

NEXT ROW: Keeping in patt, use appropriate color to purl to m, sl m, work to end with A.

Rep the last 2 rows 2 (2, 2, 2, 4, 4) more times—26 (28, 29, 30, 28, 30) sts rem.

DEC ROW 3: (RS) Keeping in patt, work to m, sl m, use appropriate color to ssk (neck dec), knit to end—1 st dec'd.

NEXT ROW: Keeping in patt, use appropriate color to purl to m, sl m, work to end with A.

Rep the last 2 rows 2 (3, 3, 3, 0, 1) more time(s)—23 (24, 25, 26, 27, 28) sts rem.

Cont even in patt until piece measures 7 (7, 7½, 7½, 8, 8)" (18 [18, 19, 19, 20.5, 20.5] cm) from dividing row, ending with a RS row.

Shape Shoulder

At armhole edge (beg of WS rows), BO 5 (5, 6, 6, 6, 7) sts 2 times, then BO 5 (6, 5, 6, 7, 6) sts once—8 edging sts rem. Place sts on holder.

Back

With RS facing, rejoin appropriate yarn to held sts, BO 4 (4, 5, 6, 6, 6) sts, knit until there are 69 (73, 76, 79, 85, 87) sts on right needle tip, turn work—69 (73, 76, 79, 85, 87) back sts; rem 37 (39, 41, 43, 45, 47) sts will be worked later for left front. Keeping in color patt, work back sts as foll:

DEC ROW 1: (WS) BO 4 (4, 5, 6, 6, 6) sts, purl to end—65 (69, 71, 73, 79, 81) sts rem.

DEC ROW 2: (RS) K2tog, knit to last 2 sts, ssk—2 sts dec'd.

Work 1 row even. Rep the last 2 rows 2 (2, 2, 2, 4, 4) more times—59 (63, 65, 67, 69, 71) sts rem. Work even in patt until piece measures 7 (7, 7½, 7½, 8, 8)" (18 [18, 19, 19, 20.5, 20.5] cm) from dividing row, ending with a WS row.

Shape Shoulders

Keeping in patt and beg with a RS row, BO 5 (5, 6, 6, 6, 7) sts at beg of next 4 rows, then BO 5 (6, 5, 6, 7, 6) sts at beg of foll 2 rows—29 (31, 31, 31, 31, 31) sts rem. BO rem sts.

Left Front

With RS facing, rejoin appropriate yarn to 37 (39, 41, 43, 45, 47) left front sts. Keeping in patt, work as foll:

DEC ROW 1: (RS) With appropriate color, BO 4 (4, 5, 6, 6, 6) sts, knit to 2 sts before m, k2tog (neck dec), sl m, with A, work in patt to end—32 (34, 35, 36, 38, 40) sts rem.

NEXT ROW: (WS) With A, work in patt to m, sl m, purl to end with appropriate color.

DEC ROW 2: With appropriate color, ssk (armhole dec), knit to 2 sts before m, k2tog (neck dec), sl m, with A, work in patt to end—2 sts dec'd.

NEXT ROW: With A, work in patt to m, sl m, purl to end with appropriate color.

Rep the last 2 rows 2 (2, 2, 2, 4, 4) more times—26 (28, 29, 30, 28, 30) sts rem.

DEC ROW 3: With appropriate color, knit to 2 sts before m, k2tog (neck nec), sl m, with A, work in patt to end—1 st dec'd.

NEXT ROW: With A, work in patt to m, sl m, purl to end with appropriate color.

Rep the last 2 rows 2 (3, 3, 3, 0, 1) more time(s)—23 (24, 25, 26, 27, 28) sts rem. Cont even in patt until piece measures 7 (7, 7½, 7½, 8, 8)" (18 [18, 19, 19, 20.5, 20.5] cm) from dividing row, ending with a WS row.

DUPLICATE-STITCH CHART

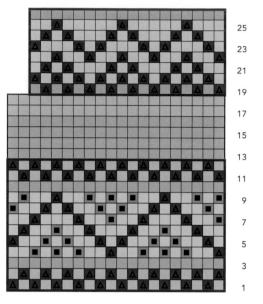

25
23
21
19
17
15
13
11
9
7
5
3
1

▲ duplicate st using A

■ duplicate st using B

☐ pattern repeat

embroidery

Chain Stitch

Bring threaded needle out from back to front, form a short loop, then insert needle backing where it came out. Keeping the loop under the needle, bring the needle back out a short distance to the right.

Cross-Stitch

Bring threaded needle out from back to front at lower left edge of the knitted stitch to be covered. Working from left to right, *insert needle at the upper right edge of the same stitch and bring it back out at the lower left edge of the adjacent stitch, directly below and in line with the insertion point. Work from right to left to work the other half of the cross.

Duplicate Stitch

Bring threaded needle out from back to front at the base of the V of the knitted stitch you want to cover. *Working right to left, pass needle in and out under the stitch in the row above it and back into the base of the same stitch. Bring needle back out at the base of the V of the next stitch to the left. Repeat from * as desired.

French Knot

Bring threaded needle out of knitted background from back to front, wrap yarn around needle three times, then use your thumb to hold the wraps in place while you insert the needle into the background a short distance from where it came out. Pull the needle through the wraps into the background to secure.

Lazy Daisy Stitch

*Bring threaded needle out of knitted background from back to front, form a short loop and insert needle into background where it came out. Keeping the loop under the needle, bring the needle back out of the background a short distance away (Figure 1), pull loop snug, and insert needle into fabric on far side of loop. Beginning each stitch at the same point in the background, repeat from * for the desired number of petals (Figure 2; 6 petals shown).

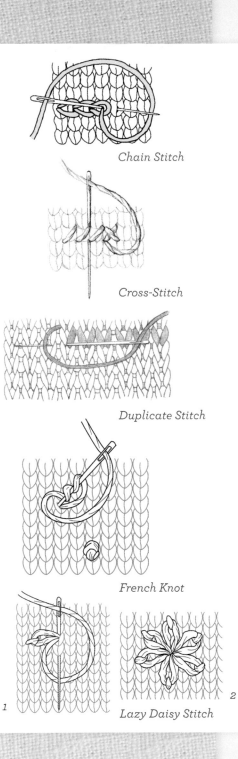

Chain Stitch

Cross-Stitch

Duplicate Stitch

French Knot

Lazy Daisy Stitch

Shape Shoulder

At armhole edge (beg of RS rows), BO 5 (5, 6, 6, 6, 7) sts 2 times, then BO 5 (6, 5, 6, 7, 6) sts once—8 edging sts rem. Place sts on holder.

Sleeves

With A and smaller needle, work picot CO as folls: *Use the cable method to CO 5 sts, BO 2 sts, slip st from right needle tip onto left needle tip (3 sts on left-hand needle); rep from * until there are 45 (45, 51, 51, 54, 54) sts, then use the cable method to CO 2 (2, 0, 0, 1, 1) more st(s)—47 (47, 51, 51, 55, 55) sts. Knit 2 rows. Work 8 rows in striped garter st (knit every row) as folls: 2 rows B, 2 rows C, 2 rows D, 2 rows B. Change to C and larger needle, and beg with a knit row, work color patt and *at the same time* inc as foll:

INC ROW: (RS) Maintaining color patt, k1, M1 (see Glossary), work in St st to last st, M1, k1—2 sts inc'd.

Work 7 rows even in patt. Rep the last 8 rows 3 more times—55 (55, 59, 59, 63, 63) sts. Work even in patt until piece measures about 14" (35.5 cm) from CO, ending with the same WS row of color patt as for body.

Shape Cap

BO 4 (4, 5, 5, 6, 6) sts at beg of next 2 rows—47 (47, 49, 49, 51, 51) sts rem.

DEC ROW 1: (RS) Ssk, knit to last 2 sts, k2tog—2 sts dec'd.

DEC ROW 2: (WS) P2tog, purl to last 2 sts ssp (see Glossary)—2 sts dec'd.

Beg with the next RS row, rep Dec Row 1 every other row 15 more times—13 (13, 15, 15, 17, 17) sts rem. BO 3 sts at beg of next 2 rows—7 (7, 9, 9, 11, 11) sts rem. BO all sts.

Finishing

Block pieces to finished measurements. With the appropriate color threaded on a tapestry needle, sew fronts to back at shoulders.

Neck Edging

With A, larger needle, RS facing, and beg at right front neck, work 8 held right front edging sts in patt as established until piece measures 3¼" (8.5 cm) from shoulder seam. Place sts on holder. Rep for left front neck. Adjust length as necessary so that edging will stand up, then use the three-needle method (see Glossary) to join left and right neck edging at center back neck. Sew selvedge edge to back neck edge.

Embroidery

With appropriate color threaded on a tapestry needle, work duplicate stitches (see page 31) according to chart on page 30 to create Fair Isle border around hem and cuffs.

With yarn threaded on a tapestry needle, sew side and sleeve seams. Sew sleeve caps into armholes, matching center of cap to shoulder seam and easing caps to fit while aligning stripes on cap and body.

FINISHED SIZE
About 36 (38, 40½, 42½, 44½, 47)" (91.5 [96.5, 103, 108, 113, 119.5] cm) bust circumference. Sweater shown measures 36" (91.5 cm).

YARN
DK weight (#3 Light).

SHOWN HERE: Louisa Harding Grace Wool and Silk (50% merino, 50% silk; 110 yd [101 m]/50 g): #20 Whale (gray, A), 10 (10, 11, 11, 12, 12) balls; #21 Rosy (B), 2 (2, 3, 3, 3, 3) balls.

NEEDLES
Body and sleeves: size U.S. 6 (4 mm).

Edging: size U.S. 3 (3.25 mm).

Adjust needle size if necessary to obtain the correct gauge.

NOTIONS
Tapestry needle; stitch holder.

GAUGE
22 stitches and 30 rows = 4" (10 cm) in stockinette stitch on larger needles.

Flora

The hem of this sweater provides a canvas for a sampler-style alphabet worked in duplicate stitch. For this design, I chose to work the embroidery in a subtle color palette, but you could get an entirely different look with bold colors. Use this alphabet chart to embroider names, words, or phrases instead on this sweater, or on any of the other projects in this chapter.

Back

With B and smaller needles, work picot CO as foll: *use the cable method (see Glossary) to CO 5 sts, BO 2 sts, return st on right-hand needle to left-hand needle (3 sts on left-hand needle); rep from * until there are 99 (105, 111, 117, 123, 129) sts. Work 2 rows in garter st (knit every row), ending with a WS row. With A, work 4 rows in garter st. Change to B and knit 1 row.

EYELET ROW: (WS) K1, p1, *yo, p2tog; rep from * to last st, k1.

Change to A and work 4 rows in garter st.

Change to larger needles. Beg with a RS row, work 16 rows in St st (knit RS rows; purl WS rows), ending with a WS row. Work 2 rows in garter st. Change to B and knit 1 row. Rep eyelet row. Change to A and work 2 rows in garter st—piece measures about 3¾" (9.5 cm) from CO. With A and beg with a RS row, work even in St st until piece measures 14 (14, 14½, 14½, 15¼, 15¼)" (35.5 [35.5, 37, 37, 38.5, 38.5] cm) from CO, ending with a WS row.

Shape Armholes

BO 4 (5, 5, 6, 6, 6) sts at beg of next 2 rows, then BO 4 (4, 5, 5, 5, 6) sts at beg of foll 2 rows—83 (87, 91, 95, 101, 105) sts rem.

DEC ROW: (RS) K3, k2tog, knit to last 5 sts, ssk, k3—2 sts dec'd.

Work 1 WS row even. Rep the last 2 rows 2 (2, 3, 4, 5, 5) more times—77 (81, 83, 85, 89, 93) sts rem. Cont even until armholes measure 6 (6, 6¼, 6¼, 6¾, 6¾)" (15 [15, 16, 16, 17, 17] cm), ending with a WS row.

Shape Neck and Shoulders

Right Shoulder

With RS facing, k18 (20, 21, 22, 24, 26), turn work; rem 59 (61, 62, 63, 65, 67) sts will be worked later for neck and other shoulder.

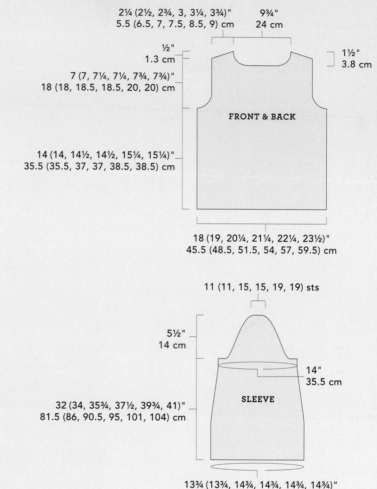

NECK DEC ROW 1: (WS) Ssp (see Glossary), purl to end—1 st dec'd.

NECK DEC ROW 2: (RS) Knit to last 2 sts, ssk—1 st dec'd.

Rep the last 2 rows 2 more times—12 (14, 15, 16, 18, 20) sts rem. Work 1 WS row even. With RS facing, BO 6 (7, 7, 8, 9, 10) sts, work to end—6 (7, 8, 8, 9, 10) sts rem. BO rem sts at beg of next RS row.

Left Shoulder

With RS facing, sl center 41 sts onto a holder for neck, rejoin yarn to rem 18 (20, 21, 22, 24, 26) sts, work to end.

NECK DEC ROW 1: (WS) Purl to last 2 sts, p2tog—1 st dec'd.

NECK DEC ROW 2: (RS) K2tog, knit to end—1 st dec'd.

Rep the previous 2 rows 2 more times—12 (14, 15, 16, 18, 20) sts rem. Work 2 rows even, ending with a RS row. With WS facing, BO 6 (7, 7, 8, 9, 10) sts, work to end—6 (7, 8, 8, 9, 10) sts rem. BO rem sts at beg of next WS row.

Front

CO and work as for back.

Sleeves

With B, smaller needles, and using the picot method as for back and front, CO 75 (75, 81, 81, 81, 81) sts. Work 2 rows in garter st, ending with a WS row. Change to A and work 4 rows in garter st. Change to B and knit 1 row.

EYELET ROW: (WS) K1, p1, *yo, p2tog; rep from * to last st, k1.

Change to A and work 4 rows in garter st. Change to larger needle and beg with a RS row, work 16 rows in St st, ending with a WS row. Work 2 rows in garter st. Change to B and knit 1 row. Rep eyelet row. Change to A and work

2 rows in garter st. Beg with a RS row, work 10 rows in St st, ending with a WS row.

DEC ROW: (RS) K3, k2tog, knit to last 5 sts, ssk, k3—2 sts dec'd.

Beg with a WS row, work 9 rows in St st. Rep the last 10 rows 1 (1, 2, 2, 0, 0) more time(s)—71 (71, 75, 75, 79, 79) sts rem. Beg with a WS row, work even in St st until piece measures 14" (35.5 cm) from CO, ending with a WS row.

Shape Cap

BO 4 sts at beg of next 2 rows, then BO 3 sts at beg of foll 2 rows—57 (57, 61, 61, 65, 65) sts rem.

DEC ROW 1: (RS) Ssk, knit to last 2 sts, k2tog—2 sts dec'd.

DEC ROW 2: (WS) P2tog, purl to last 2 sts, ssp—2 sts dec'd.

Beg with the next RS row, rep Dec Row 1 every other row 3 more times, every foll 4th row 5 times, then every other row 2 times—33 (33, 37, 37, 41, 41) sts rem. Work Dec Row 2, then Dec Row 1, then work Dec Row 2 once more—27 (27, 31, 31, 35, 35) sts rem. BO 4 sts at beg of next 4 rows—11 (11, 15, 15, 19, 19) sts rem. BO all sts.

Finishing

Weave in loose ends. Block pieces to finished measurements.

Embellishment

With B threaded on a tapestry needle, use duplicate sts (see page 31) to embroider your choice of letters from the Alphabet chart (see page 38) around the lower body edge. Embroider heart motifs on the sleeves or use the alphabet letters to embroider names, sayings, or phrases.

Neck Edging

With yarn threaded on a tapestry needle, sew right shoulder seam.

ALPHABET CHART

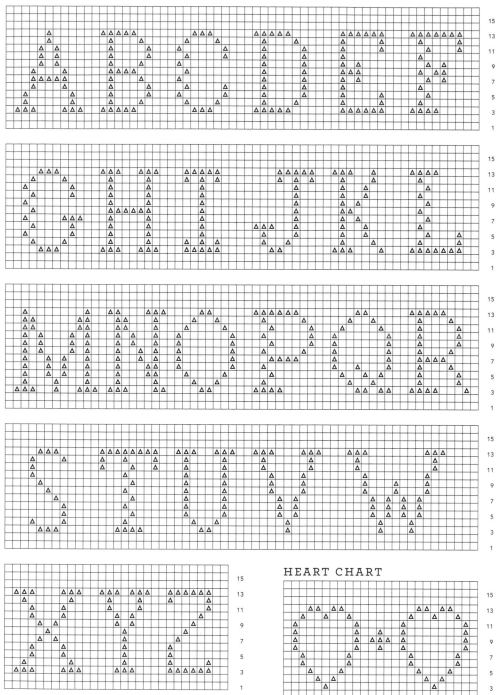

HEART CHART

☐ Background color

△ Contrast color

With A, smaller needles, RS facing, and beg at left front neck edge, pick up and knit 10 sts along left front neck, k41 held front neck sts, pick up and knit 10 sts to shoulder, 9 sts along right back neck, k41 held back neck sts, and pick up and knit 10 sts along left back neck to shoulder—121 sts total. Knit 1 WS row. Change to B and knit 1 RS row.

EYELET ROW: (WS) K1, p1, *yo, p2tog; rep from * to last st, k1.

Change to A and work 3 rows in garter st, ending with a RS row. With WS facing, BO all sts kwise.

Seams

With A threaded on a tapestry needle, sew left shoulder and neck edging seam. Sew side seams. Sew sleeve seams. Sew sleeve caps into armholes, matching center of cap to shoulder seam and easing caps to fit.

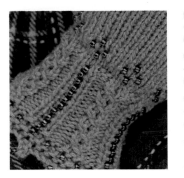

beading

Beads are a beautiful yet simple way to add interest to any knitted piece. This chapter shows how to knit with beads in a variety of patterns. There are two variations of the lace scarf Clarissa (page 56)—one with a tonal effect of beads in the allover lace pattern and another with clear glass beads that shimmer at every turn. The simple Talullah (page 46) bolero is made elegant by a beaded lace edging. Prudence (page 60), a pair of fingerless mittens, is a quick project perfected with a beaded cast-on and bind-off. Both the Verity evening purse (page 42) and Constance beret (page 52) use charts to illustrate the bead placements. Beads at the edgings highlight the simple allover lace pattern in Bettine (page 64), making this shrug look far more complicated to make than it is.

FINISHED SIZE
About 8" (20.5 cm) wide and 9" (23 cm) long.

YARN
DK weight (#3 Light).

SHOWN HERE: Louisa Harding Kashmir DK (55% wool, 10% cashmere, 35% microfiber; 116 yd [106 m]/50 g): #33 Dove, 2 balls.

NEEDLES
Size U.S. 6 (4 mm).

Adjust needle size if necessary to obtain the correct gauge.

NOTIONS
Beading needle; 192 size 6° pewter gray beads; tapestry needle; 7" (18 cm) round-top purse clasp with holes; coordinating felt measuring 7½" (19 cm) wide and 18" (45.5 cm) long for lining; sharp-point sewing needle and matching thread.

GAUGE
22 stitches and 30 rows = 4" (10 cm) in stockinette stitch.

Verity

This purse design came about in my desire to use a lovely clasp that I found in a little haberdashery shop on my travels. I knitted the front and back in a simple beaded fabric, then sewed the two pieces together along the sides and bottom and attached the clasp to the top. I added a lining for stability. The gray tones mix together with the silver clasp in a sophisticated bag with a vintage heirloom quality.

43

Stitch Guide

Bead 1 (worked on RS rows)

With RS facing, bring yarn to front (RS of work) slide a bead next to the st just worked, sl 1 pwise, bring yarn to back (WS of work), leaving bead in front of slipped st. The bead will be secured when the next st is knitted.

Note

Before beginning, thread the knitting yarn on a beading needle, then thread the desired number of beads onto the yarn.

BEADED LACE CHART

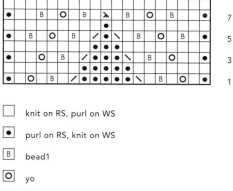

☐ knit on RS, purl on WS

▣ purl on RS, knit on WS

B bead1

O yo

\ ssk

/ k2tog

⋏ sl 1, k2tog, psso

Bag Back

CO 47 sts. Work 4 rows in garter st (knit every row).

ROW 1: (RS) K14, work Row 1 of Beaded Lace chart across 19 sts, k14.

ROW 2: (WS) K1, p13, work Row 2 chart across 19 sts, p13, k1.

ROWS 3–8: Cont as established through Row 8 of chart.

ROWS 9–16: Rep Rows 1–8.

ROW 17: K3, ssk, k9, work Row 1 of chart across 19 sts, k9, k2tog, k3—45 sts rem.

ROW 18: K1, p12, work Row 2 of chart across 19 sts, p12, k1.

ROW 19: K13, work Row 3 of chart across 19 sts, k13.

ROW 20: K1, p12, work Row 4 of chart across 19 sts, p12, k1.

ROWS 21–32: Work 12 rows even in patt as established.

ROW 33: K3, ssk, k8, work Row 1 of chart across 19 sts, k8, k2tog, k3—43 sts rem.

ROW 34: K1, p11, work Row 2 of chart across 19 sts, p11, k1.

ROW 35: K12, work Row 3 of chart across 19 sts, k12.

ROW 36: K1, p11, work Row 4 of chart across 19 sts, p11, p1.

ROWS 37–48: Work 12 rows even in patt as established.

ROW 49: K3, ssk, k7, work Row 1 of chart across 19 sts, k7, k2tog, k3—41 sts rem.

ROW 50: K1, p10, work Row 2 of chart across 19 sts, p10, k1.

ROW 51: K11, work Row 3 of chart across 19 sts, k11.

ROW 52: K1, p10, work Row 4 of chart across 19 sts, p10, k1.

ROWS 53–64: Work 12 rows even in patt as established, ending with Row 8 of chart.

Work 2 rows even in St st (knit RS rows; purl WS rows). BO all sts.

Bag Front

CO and work as for back.

Finishing

Weave in loose ends. Block to finished measurements.

Assembly

With yarn threaded on a tapestry needle and RS of CO edge tog, use a whipstitch (see Glossary) to form a fold line. With WS tog, fold piece in half along bottom fold line. Mark position of purse handles on side seams. With yarn threaded on a tapestry needle, use a mattress st (see Glossary) to sew sides from base to marked handle positions. With strong sewing thread, attach purse clasp to knitted fabric.

Lining

Note: You may need to adapt the lining to match the shape of your purse clasp.

Fold lining fabric in half width wise with WS tog. With matching thread and sewing needle, use a backstitch (see Glossary) with a ⅜" (1 cm) seam allowance to sew side seams. Slip lining inside knitted bag, turn ⅜" (1 cm) under at top edge, and use whipstitches (see Glossary) to secure just below CO edge.

FINISHED SIZE
About 35½ (36¾, 39½, 41½, 43½, 44¾)" (90 [93.5, 100.5, 105.5, 110.5, 113.5] cm) bust circumference. Bolero shown measures 35½" (90 cm).

YARN
Worsted weight (#4 Medium).

SHOWN HERE: Louisa Harding Grace (50% merino, 50% silk; 110 yd [100 m]/50 g): #22 Reflection (light blue), 6 (7, 7, 8, 8, 9) balls.

NEEDLES
Size U.S. 7 (4.5 mm).

Adjust needle size if necessary to obtain the correct gauge.

NOTIONS
About 520 (550, 580, 610, 640, 670) size 6° clear silver-lined beads; small-eye needle for threading beads; tapestry needle.

GAUGE
20 stitches and 28 rows = 4" (10 cm) in stockinette stitch.

Talullah

A stunning beaded edging transforms this short-sleeved bolero into a dazzling garment suitable for the opera. The body is worked first in stockinette stitch, then the edging is worked separately in a lovely lace pattern that is accented with beads. The beads are threaded onto the yarn before starting, then secured in place with simple slip stitches as the lace pattern is worked. The look is beautiful and elegant, and the pattern, with practice, is easy to work.

Stitch Guide

Bead 1 (worked on RS rows)

With RS facing, bring yarn to front (RS) of work, slip a bead next to the stitch just worked, slip the next stitch purlwise, bring yarn to back (WS) of work (bead will sit in front of slipped st)—the bead will be secured when the next stitch is worked.

Notes

Before starting, thread the beads onto the knitting yarn. To do this, thread the yarn on a small-eye needle that will easily pass through the center of the beads, thread the appropriate number of beads onto the yarn.

In this pattern, 13 beads are used for each lace pattern repeat. When working the bolero edging, thread on enough beads to work 10 pattern repeats (this will enable the yarn to move freely through the beads). At the end of these repeats, cut yarn and thread on enough beads for the next 10 repeats.

Each sleeve edging has 6 pattern repeats, which requires 78 beads.

Back

CO 79 (83, 89, 95, 99, 103) sts. Beg with a RS row, work 8 rows in St st (knit RS rows; purl WS rows).

INC ROW: (RS) K3, M1 (see Glossary), knit to last 3 sts, M1, K3—2 sts inc'd.

Work 7 rows even in St st. Rep the last 8 rows 3 times—87 (91, 97, 103, 107, 111) sts. Cont even in St st until piece measures 6½ (6½, 7, 7, 7¾, 7¾)" (16.5 [16.5, 18, 18, 19.5, 19.5] cm) from CO, ending with a WS row.

Shape Armholes

BO 4 (5, 7, 8, 9, 10) sts at beg of next 2 rows,

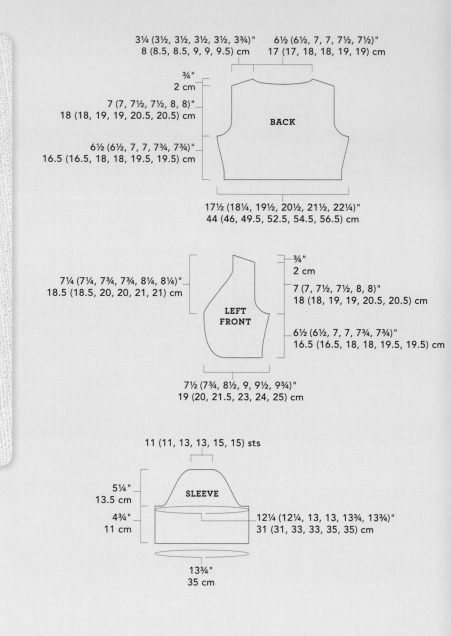

3¼ (3½, 3½, 3½, 3½, 3¾)"
8 (8.5, 8.5, 9, 9, 9.5) cm

6½ (6½, 7, 7, 7½, 7½)"
17 (17, 18, 18, 19, 19) cm

¾"
2 cm

7 (7, 7½, 7½, 8, 8)"
18 (18, 19, 19, 20.5, 20.5) cm

BACK

6½ (6½, 7, 7, 7¾, 7¾)"
16.5 (16.5, 18, 18, 19.5, 19.5) cm

17½ (18¼, 19½, 20½, 21½, 22¼)"
44 (46, 49.5, 52.5, 54.5, 56.5) cm

7¼ (7¼, 7¾, 7¾, 8¼, 8¼)"
18.5 (18.5, 20, 20, 21, 21) cm

¾"
2 cm

7 (7, 7½, 7½, 8, 8)"
18 (18, 19, 19, 20.5, 20.5) cm

LEFT FRONT

6½ (6½, 7, 7, 7¾, 7¾)"
16.5 (16.5, 18, 18, 19.5, 19.5) cm

7½ (7¾, 8½, 9, 9½, 9¾)"
19 (20, 21.5, 23, 24, 25) cm

11 (11, 13, 13, 15, 15) sts

5¼"
13.5 cm

SLEEVE

4¾"
11 cm

12¼ (12¼, 13, 13, 13¾, 13¾)"
31 (31, 33, 33, 35, 35) cm

13¾"
35 cm

then BO 3 (3, 3, 4, 4, 4) sts at beg of 2 foll rows—73 (75, 77, 79, 81, 83) sts rem.

DEC ROW: (RS) K3, k2tog, knit to last 5 sts, ssk, k3—2 sts dec'd.

Purl 1 WS row. Rep the last 2 rows 3 more times—65 (67, 69, 71, 73, 75) sts rem. Cont even until armholes measure 7 (7, 7½, 7½, 8, 8)" (18 [18, 19, 19, 20.5, 20.5] cm), ending with a WS row.

Shape Shoulders and Neck

BO 5 (6, 6, 6, 6, 6) sts at beg of next 2 rows—55 (55, 57, 59, 61, 63) sts rem.

Right Shoulder

With RS facing, BO 5 (6, 6, 6, 6, 6) sts, knit until there are 9 (8, 8, 9, 9, 10) sts on right-hand needle, turn work—rem 41 (41, 43, 44, 46, 47) sts will be worked later for left shoulder and neck. With WS facing, work 9 (8, 8, 9, 9, 10) right shoulder sts as foll: BO 3 sts, purl to end—6 (5, 5, 6, 6, 7) sts rem. BO rem sts.

Left Shoulder

With RS facing, rejoin yarn to rem sts, BO center 27 (27, 29, 29, 31, 31) sts, knit to end—14 (14, 14, 15, 15, 16) sts rem. With WS facing, BO 5 (6, 6, 6, 6, 6) sts, purl to end—9 (8, 8, 9, 9, 10) sts rem. With RS facing, BO 3 sts, knit to end—6 (5, 5, 6, 6, 7) sts rem. BO rem sts.

Left Front

CO 24 (26, 29, 32, 34, 36) sts. Inc along center front edge as foll:

ROW 1: (RS) Knit.

ROW 2: (WS) K1f&b (see Glossary), purl to end—1 st inc'd.

ROW 3: Knit to last st, k1f&b—1 st inc'd.

ROW 4: K1f&b, purl to end—1 st inc'd.

ROWS 5 AND 7: Knit to last st, k1f&b—29 (31, 34, 37, 39, 41) sts after Row 7.

ROWS 6, 8, 10, 12, 14, AND 16: Purl.

ROW 9: (inc at side and center front edges) K3, M1, knit to last st, k1f&b—2 sts inc'd.

ROWS 11, 13, AND 15: Knit to last st, k1f&b—34 (36, 39, 42, 44, 46) sts after Row 15.

ROW 17: (RS) K3, M1, knit to end—1 st inc'd.

Beg with a WS row, work 7 rows even in St st. Rep the last 8 rows 2 more times—37 (39, 42, 45, 47, 49) sts. Work even in St st until piece measures 6½ (6½, 7, 7, 7¾, 7¾)" (16.5 [16.5, 18, 18, 19.5, 19.5] cm) from CO, ending with a WS row.

Shape Armhole and Neck

At armhole edge (beg of RS rows), BO 4 (5, 7, 8, 9, 10) sts once, then BO 3 (3, 3, 4, 4, 4) sts once—30 (31, 32, 33, 34, 35) sts rem. Work 1 WS row even. Dec as foll:

ROW 1: (RS) K3, k2tog, knit to last 5 sts, ssk, k3—2 sts dec'd.

ROWS 2 AND 4: Purl.

ROW 3: K3, k2tog, knit to end—1 st dec'd.

Rep these 4 rows once more—24 (25, 26, 27, 28, 29) sts rem. Rep Row 3, then work 3 rows even—1 st dec'd. Rep the last 4 rows 7 (7, 8, 8, 9, 9) more times—16 (17, 17, 18, 18, 19) sts rem. Work even in St st until armhole measures 7 (7, 7½, 7½, 8, 8)" (18 [18, 19, 19, 20.5, 20.5] cm), ending with a WS row.

Shape Shoulder

At armhole edge, BO 5 (6, 6, 6, 6, 6) sts 2 times—6 (5, 5, 6, 6, 7) sts rem. At beg of next RS row, BO all sts.

Right Front

CO 24 (26, 29, 32, 34, 36) sts. Inc along center front edge as foll:

ROW 1: (RS) Knit.

ROW 2: (WS) Purl to last st, k1f&b—1 st inc'd.

ROW 3: K1f&b, knit to end—1 st inc'd.

ROW 4: Purl to last st, k1f&b—1 st inc'd.

ROWS 5 AND 7: K1f&b, knit to end—29 (31, 34, 37, 39, 41) sts after Row 7.

ROWS 6, 8, 10, 12, 14, AND 16: Purl.

ROW 9: (inc at side and center front edges) K1f&b, knit to last 3 sts, M1, k3—2 sts inc'd.

ROWS 11, 13, AND 15: K1f&b, knit to end—34 (36, 39, 42, 44, 46) after Row 15.

ROW 17: Knit to last 3 sts, M1, k3—1 st inc'd.

Beg with a WS row, work 7 rows even in St st, ending with a WS row. Rep the last 8 rows 2 more times—37 (39, 42, 45, 47, 49) sts. Work even in St st until piece measures 6½ (6½, 7, 7, 7¾, 7¾)" (16.5 [16.5, 18, 18, 19.5, 19.5] cm) from CO, ending with a RS row.

Shape Armhole and Neck

At armhole edge (beg of WS rows), BO 4 (5, 7, 8, 9, 10) sts once, then BO 3 (3, 3, 4, 4, 4) sts once—30 (31, 32, 33, 34, 35) sts rem. Dec as foll:

ROW 1: (RS) K3, k2tog, knit to last 5 sts, ssk, k3—2 sts dec'd.

ROWS 2 AND 4: Purl.

ROW 3: Knit to last 5 sts, ssk, k3—1 st dec'd.

Rep these 4 rows once more—24 (25, 26, 27, 28, 29) sts rem. Rep Row 3, then work 3 rows even—1 st dec'd. Rep the last 4 rows 7 (7, 8, 8, 9, 9) more times—16 (17, 17, 18, 18, 19) sts rem. Work even in St st until armhole measures 7 (7, 7½, 7½, 8, 8)" (18 [18, 19, 19, 20.5, 20.5] cm), ending with a RS row.

Shape Shoulder

At armhole edge, BO 5 (6, 6, 6, 6, 6) sts 2 times—6 (5, 5, 6, 6, 7) sts rem. At beg of next WS row, BO rem sts.

LACE AND BEAD CHART

☐	knit on RS, purl on WS
●	purl on RS, knit on WS
+	CO
▬	slide a bead up to work
⌒	BO
╱	k2tog
╲	ssk
O	yo
B	bead1
⋏	sl 1, k2tog, psso
■	no stitch

DEC ROW 2: (WS) Ssp (see Glossary), purl to last 2 sts, p2tog—2 sts dec'd.

Rep the last 2 rows once more—43 (43, 45, 45, 47, 47) sts rem.

[Rep Dec Row 1, work 1 WS row even] 2 times, rep Dec Row 1 once again—37 (37, 39, 39, 41, 41) sts rem.

[Work 3 rows even, ending with a WS row. Rep Dec Row 1] 4 times—29 (29, 31, 31, 33, 33) sts rem.

[Work 1 WS row even, work Dec Row 1] 3 times—23 (23, 25, 25, 27, 27) sts rem.

BO 3 sts beg of next 4 rows—11 (11, 13, 13, 15, 15) sts rem. BO all sts.

Finishing

Block pieces to finished measurements. With yarn threaded on a tapestry needle and using a backstitch (see Glossary) sew fronts to back at shoulders. Use a mattress st (see Glossary) to sew side seams.

Body Edging

Thread appropriate number of beads onto working yarn (see Notes). CO 15 sts.

FOUNDATION ROW 1: Knit.

FOUNDATION ROW 2: K2, p11, k2.

Rep Rows 1–16 of Lace and Bead chart until piece is long enough to fit around center edge of bolero, beg at right side seam, up around right front, across back neck, down left front to left side seam, and across bottom edge of back, ending with a RS row. With WS facing, BO all sts knitwise.

With yarn threaded on a tapestry needle, whipstitch (see Glossary) edging in place, easing as necessary around curves.

Sew sleeve seams. Sew sleeve caps into armholes, easing as necessary. Weave in loose ends.

Sleeves

Thread 78 beads onto working yarn.

Edging

CO 15 sts.

FOUNDATION ROW 1: (RS) Knit.

FOUNDATION ROW 2: K2, p11, k2.

Work Rows 1–16 of Lace and Bead chart 6 times—piece measures about 13¾" (35 cm) from CO.

Sleeve Body

Turn edging 45 degrees clockwise so that the left-hand selvedge is at the top. With RS facing and yarn still attached, pick up and knit 61 (61, 65, 65, 69, 69) sts along the top of edging. Beg with WS row, work 9 rows in St st, ending with a WS row.

Shape Cap

BO 5 (5, 6, 6, 7, 7) sts at beg of next 2 rows—51 (51, 53, 53, 55, 55) sts rem.

DEC ROW 1: (RS) K2tog, knit to last 2 sts, ssk—2 sts dec'd.

FINISHED SIZE
About 20" (51 cm) head circumference, stretched.

To fit an average-size female.

YARN
Worsted weight (#4 Medium).

SHOWN HERE: Louisa Harding Thistle (60% merino, 40% suri alpaca; 98 yd [90 m]/50 g): #16 Surf, 2 balls.

NEEDLES
Sides and brim: size U.S. 8 (5 mm).

Edging: size U.S. 6 (4 mm).

Adjust needle size if necessary to obtain the correct gauge.

NOTIONS
Beading needle; 442 size 6° silver-lined clear beads; tapestry needle.

GAUGE
18 stitches and 24 rows = 4" (10 cm) in stockinette stitch on larger needles.

Constance

A row of beaded hearts provides stability and elegant sparkle to the brim of this feminine beret. If you've never before incorporated beads in your knitting, this beret is a great place to start. The pattern is simple to follow and the project is small enough to finish in just a few hours. Knit one for someone close to your heart.

Stitch Guide

Bead 1 (worked on RS rows)

With RS facing, bring yarn to front (RS of work) slide a bead next to the st just worked, sl 1 pwise, bring yarn to back (WS of work), leaving bead in front of slipped st. The bead will be secured when the next st is knitted.

Note

Before beginning, thread the knitting yarn on a beading needle, then thread the desired number of beads onto the yarn.

BEADED HEART CHART

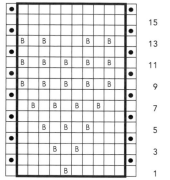

- □ knit on RS, purl on WS
- ⊡ purl on RS, knit on WS
- B bead 1
- ▢ pattern repeat

Beret

With smaller needles, CO 93 sts. Work beaded rib as foll:

ROW 1: (RS) *K2, p1, k1, bead 1 (see Stitch Guide), k1, p1; rep from * to last 2 sts, k2.

ROW 2: (WS) K1, *p1, k1, p3, k1, p1; rep from * to last st, k1.

Rep these 2 rows 9 more times, ending with a WS row.

INC ROW: (RS) [K1, M1 (see Glossary)] 2 times, [k5, (M1, k1) 2 times, M1] 12 times, k5, M1, k2—132 sts.

NEXT ROW: (WS) K1, purl to last st, k1.

Change to larger needles. Work Rows 1–16 of Beaded Heart chart—piece measures about 4½" (11.5 cm) from CO.

Shape Top

DEC ROW 1: (RS) K1, *ssk, k6, k2tog; rep from * to last st, k1—106 sts rem.

Knitting the first and last st of every row, work 7 rows even in St st (knit RS rows; purl WS rows).

DEC ROW 2: K1, *ssk, k4, k2tog; rep from * to last st, k1—80 sts rem.

Knitting the first and last st of every row, work 3 rows even in St st.

DEC ROW 3: K1, *ssk, k2, k2tog; rep from * to last st, k1—54 sts rem.

Knitting the first and last st of every row, work 3 rows even in St st.

DEC ROW 4: K1, *ssk, k2tog; rep from * to last st, k1—28 sts rem.

NEXT ROW: (WS) K1, purl to last st, k1.

DEC ROW 5: K1, *ssk; rep from * to last st, k1—15 sts rem.

NEXT ROW: K1, purl to last st, k1.

Cut yarn leaving a 6" (15 cm) tail, thread through rem sts, pull tight, and fasten off to WS.

Finishing

Weave in loose ends. Block to finished measurements. With yarn threaded on a tapestry needle, use a mattress st or backstitch (see Glossary) to sew edges tog, working the garter selvedge st into the seam allowance.

FINISHED SIZE
Merletto version: about 11½"
(29 cm) wide and 39½" (100.5 cm)
long.

Mulberry Silk version: about 10"
(25.5 cm) wide and 72½"
(184 cm) long.

YARN
DK weight (#3 Light).

SHOWN HERE: Louisa Harding
Merletto (46% viscose, 34% nylon,
20% linen; 98 yd [90 m]/50 g): #17
True (navy), 4 balls.

Louisa Harding Mulberry Silk (100%
silk; 136 yd [124 m]/50 g): #32 Lapis
(purple), 5 balls.

NEEDLES
Body: size U.S. 7 (4.5 mm).

Edging: size U.S. 6 (4 mm).

*Adjust needle size if necessary to
obtain the correct gauge.*

NOTIONS
874 size 6° frosted blue glass
beads for Merletto scarf; 1,714 size
6° silver-lined clear glass beads
for Mulberry Silk scarf; beading
needle; tapestry needle.

GAUGE
Merletto version: 18 stitches and 24
rows = 4" (10 cm) in lace pattern
on larger needles.

Mulberry Silk version: 20 stitches
and 28 rows = 4" (10 cm) in lace
pattern on larger needles.

Clarissa

Nothing speaks elegance and sophistication like a simple beaded scarf. For fun, I've shown this design worked in two different
yarns—one in Merletto, a blend of viscose, nylon, and linen, and
the other in Mulberry Silk (page 58), a pure silk yarn. I chose
muted frosted beads on one scarf to lend a subtle weight and
drape and silver-lined beads on the other to catch the light and
the attention of onlookers.

Merletto version.

Stitch Guide

Bead 1 (worked on RS rows)

With RS facing, bring yarn to front (RS of work) slide a bead next to the st just worked, sl 1 pwise, bring yarn to back (WS of work), leaving bead in front of slipped st. The bead will be secured when the next st is knitted.

Notes

Before beginning, thread the knitting yarn on a beading needle, then thread the desired number of beads onto the yarn.

Each pattern repeat uses 105 beads. Thread enough beads for two pattern repeats so that the yarn can move freely through the beads. At the end of the two repeats, cut the yarn and thread enough beads for two more repeats. Weave in the loose ends when finishing the scarf.

Mulberry Silk version.

BEADED DIAMONDS CHART

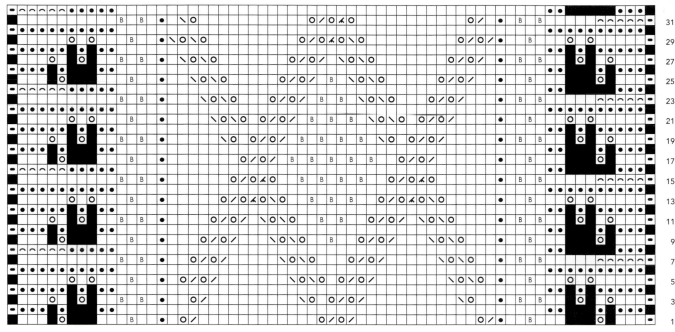

knit on RS, purl on WS

● purl on RS, knit on WS

– slip a bead up to work

O yo

B bead 1

／ k2tog

＼ ssk

⌒ BO

⊀ k3tog

■ no stitch

Scarf

With smaller needles, work beaded picot CO as folls: *Use the cable method (see Glossary) to CO 5 sts, slide a bead up to work, BO 2 sts, return st on right-hand needle to left-hand needle (3 sts on left-hand needle); rep from * 16 more times, use the cable method to CO 2 more sts—53 sts total. Work 4 rows in garter st (knit every row).

Change to larger needles. Work Rows 1–32 of Beaded Diamonds chart 8 times for Merletto scarf and 16 times for Mulberry Silk scarf. Change to smaller needle and work 4 rows in garter st, ending with a WS row.

With RS facing, work beaded picot BO as folls: *sl st on right-hand needle onto left-hand needle, use the cable method to CO 2 sts, slide bead up to work, BO 5 sts; rep from * 17 more times, BO to end.

Finishing

Weave in loose ends. Block to finished measurements.

FINISHED SIZE
About 8" (20.5 cm) hand circumference.

YARN
DK weight (#3 Light).

SHOWN HERE: Louisa Harding
Kashmir DK (55% merino, 35%
microfiber, 10% cashmere; 116 yd
[106 m]/50 g): #35 Spruce, 2 balls.

NEEDLES
Hand: size U.S. 6 (4 mm).

Edging: size U.S. 3 (3.25 mm).

*Adjust needle size if necessary to
obtain the correct gauge.*

NOTIONS
Beading needle; 284 size 6° bronze
beads; stitch holder; tapestry
needle.

GAUGE
22 stitches and 30 rows = 4"
(10 cm) in stockinette stitch on
larger needles.

Prudence

These fingerless mittens are fast and fun to knit with beads
in the cast-on and bind-off edges. The combination of bronze
beads and the green yarn reminds me of *verdigris*, the green
coating or patina formed when copper, brass, or bronze is
weathered. The simple embellished edging detail is probably
the easiest way to learn bead knitting.

Stitch Guide

Bead 1

On RS rows: Bring yarn to front (RS of work) slide a bead next to the st just worked, sl 1 pwise, bring yarn to back (WS of work), leaving bead in front of slipped st. The bead will be secured when the next st is worked.

On WS rows: Bring yarn to back (RS of work) slide a bead next to the st just worked, sl 1 pwise, bring yarn to front (WS of work), leaving bead in front of slipped st. The bead will be secured when the next st is worked.

Note

Before beginning, thread the knitting yarn on a beading needle, then thread the desired number of beads onto the yarn—each mitten requires 142 beads.

Right Mitten

With smaller needles, work beaded picot CO as folls: *Use the cable method (see Glossary) to CO 5 sts, slide a bead up to work, BO 2 sts, sl st on right-hand needle to left-hand needle (3 sts on left-hand needle); rep from * 12 more times (39 sts on needle), use the cable method to CO 2 more sts—41 sts total.

Cuff

Work 3 rows in garter st (knit every row).

BEAD ROW: (WS) K1, p1, *bead 1 (see Stitch Guide), p1; rep from * last st, k1.

Knit 1 RS row.

INC ROW: (WS) K1, M1 (see Glossary), knit to end—42 sts.

Work Rows 1–4 of Rib chart 5 times, then work Rows 1 and 2 once more—piece measures about 3" (7.5 cm) from CO.

Hand

Change to larger needles. Work Rows 1–10 of Hand chart.

Shape Thumb

ROW 1: (RS) K21, M1, p7, M1, k14—44 sts.

ROWS 2, 4, 6, 8, 10, AND 12: (WS) K1, purl to last st, k1.

ROWS 3 AND 5: Knit.

ROW 7: K21, M1, p9, M1, k14—46 sts.

ROW 9: K21, M1, p11, M1, k14—48 sts.

ROW 11: K22, sl next 11 sts on a holder to work later for thumb, knit to end—37 sts rem.

ROW 13: Knit.

ROW 14: K1, purl to last st, k1.

Rep the last 2 rows 8 more times, ending with a WS row.

Change to smaller needles. Work 3 rows even in garter st.

BEAD ROW: (WS) K1, p1 *bead 1, p1; rep from * to last st, k1.

Work 3 rows even in garter st, ending with a RS row.

With WS facing, use the beaded picot method to BO as foll: BO 3 sts, *sl st on right-hand needle onto left-hand needle, use the cable method to CO 2 sts, slide bead up to work, BO 5 sts; rep from * 10 more times.

Thumb

Return 11 held thumb sts to larger needles and rejoin yarn with RS facing.

INC ROW: (WS) Purl into front and back of next st (p1f&b), p9, p1f&b—13 sts.

Work 4 rows even in St st, ending with a WS row.

Change to smaller needles. Work 3 rows even in garter st, ending with a RS row.

BEAD ROW: (WS) P1, *bead 1, p1; rep from *.

Knit 1 RS row. With WS facing, BO all sts kwise.

Left Mitten

CO and work as for right mitten to start of thumb shaping.

Shape Thumb

ROW 1: K14, M1, p7, M1, k21—44 sts.

ROWS 2, 4, 6, 8, 10, AND 12: (WS) K1, purl to last st, k1.

ROWS 3 AND 7: Knit.

ROW 5: K14, M1, p9, M1, k21—46 sts.

ROW 9: K14, M1, p11, M1, K21—48 sts.

ROW 11: K15, sl next 11 sts on a holder for thumb, knit to end—37 sts rem.

ROW 13: Knit.

ROW 14: K1, purl to last st, k1.

Rep the last 2 rows 8 more times, ending with a WS row.

Cont as for right mitten.

Thumb

Work as for right mitten.

Finishing

Weave in loose ends. Block to finished measurements. With yarn threaded on a tapestry needle, use a mattress st or backstitch (see Glossary) to sew side seams, working each selvedge st into the seam. Sew thumb seam, making sure that the base of the thumb is joined securely to the hand.

RIB CHART

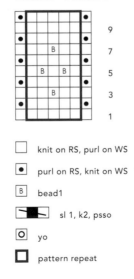

HAND CHART

☐ knit on RS, purl on WS

• purl on RS, knit on WS

B bead1

sl 1, k2, psso

O yo

☐ pattern repeat

FINISHED SIZE
About 34 (36½, 39, 41, 43½, 46)"
(86.5 [92.5, 99, 104, 110.5, 117] cm)
shoulder circumference. Shrug
shown measures 34" (86.5 cm).

Note: To measure circumference,
place measuring tape at nape of
neck, bring it to the front over
one shoulder, then wrap it below
the underarm to the back, bring it
across the back below the underarm to the front, then up over the
shoulder to the nape of the neck.

YARN
Worsted weight (#4 Medium).

SHOWN HERE: Louisa Harding
Grace (50% merino, 50% silk; 110 yd
[101 m]/50 g): #20 Whale, 4 (4, 5, 5,
6, 6) balls.

NEEDLES
Body: size U.S. 7 (4.5 mm).

Edging: size U.S. 4 (3.5 mm).

*Adjust needle size if necessary to
obtain the correct gauge.*

NOTIONS
Beading needle; markers (m);
tapestry needle; 524 (557, 590, 701,
738, 775) size 6° metallic green
beads.

GAUGE
20 stitches and 32 rows = 4" (10 cm)
in eyelet pattern on larger needles.

Bettine

The shrug is the most versatile of knitted garments—it can be
worn over most any outfit to provide a bit of warmth and style.
Because shrugs have little shaping and knit up quickly, they
are easy enough for even beginning knitters. To add simple
elegance to this design, I intertwined pretty beads in the lace
pattern. Wear this shrug with anything from jeans and a T-shirt
to a pretty summer dress.

Stitch Guide

Bead 1 (worked on WS rows)

With WS facing, bring yarn to back (RS of work) slide a bead next to the st just worked, sl 1 pwise, bring yarn to front (WS of work), leaving bead in front of slipped st. The bead will be secured when the next st is knitted.

Note

Before beginning, thread the knitting yarn on a beading needle, then thread the desired number of beads onto the yarn.

17 (18¼, 19½, 20½, 21¾, 23)"
43 (46.5, 49.5, 52, 55, 58.5) cm — 3½" / 9 cm

SHRUG

13¼ (13¼, 13¼, 15¼, 15¼, 15¼)"
34 (34, 34, 39, 39, 39) cm

24 (25¼, 26½, 27½, 28¾, 30)"
61 (64.5, 67.5, 70, 73, 76.5) cm

Shrug

With smaller needles and using the cable method (see Glossary), CO 18 sts, then work beaded picot CO as foll: *use the cable method to CO 5 sts, slide a bead up to work, BO 2 sts, return st on right-hand needle to left-hand needle; rep from * 27 (29, 31, 33, 35, 37) more times, use the cable method to CO 19 more sts—121 (127, 133, 139, 145, 151) sts. Work 3 rows in garter st (knit every row).

BEAD ROW: (WS) K18, place marker (pm), [p1, bead 1 (see Stitch Guide)] 42 (45, 48, 51, 54, 57) times, p1, pm, k18.

NEXT 2 ROWS: K18, slip marker (sl m), knit to next m, sl m, k18.

Change to larger needle. Work 8 rows in eyelet patt as foll (the pattern is charted on page 67):

ROW 1: (RS) Slide a bead up to start of work, k3, yo, k4, yo, k2tog, k9, sl m, k1, *k2tog, yo, k1, yo, ssk, k1; rep from * to next m, sl m, k10, yo, k2tog, k3, yo, k3—123 (129, 135, 141, 147, 153) sts.

ROW 2: (WS) Slide a bead up to start of work, k8, yo, k2tog, k9, sl m, purl to next m, sl m, k10, yo, k2tog, k7.

BEADED LACE CHART

Legend:

☐	knit on RS, purl on WS
●	purl on RS, knit on WS
▬	slide a bead up to work
⌒	BO
╱	k2tog
╲	ssk
O	yo
B	bead1
⅄	sl 1, k2tog, psso
■	no stitch
☐	pattern repeat
ǀ	sl m

ROW 3: Slide a bead up to start of work, k3, yo, k1, yo, k4, yo, k2tog, k9, sl m, k2tog, yo, k3, yo, *sl 1, k2tog, psso, yo, k3, yo; rep from * to 2 sts before next m, ssk, sl m, k10, yo, k2tog, k3, yo, k1, yo, k3—127 (133, 139, 145, 151, 157) sts.

ROW 4: Slide a bead up to start of work, k10, yo, k2tog, k9, sl m, p3, *bead 1, p5; rep from * to 4 sts before next m, bead 1, p3, sl m, k10, yo, k2tog, k9.

ROW 5: Slide a bead up to start of work, k5, yo, k1, yo, k4, yo, k2tog, k9, sl m, k1, *yo, ssk, k1, k2tog, yo, k1; rep from * to next m, sl m, k10, yo, k2tog, k3, yo, k1, yo, k5—131 (137, 143, 149, 155, 161) sts.

ROW 6: Slide a bead up to start of work, k12, yo, k2tog, k9, sl m, purl to next m, sl m, k10, yo, k2tog, k11.

ROW 7: Slide a bead up to start of work, BO 5 sts (1 st on right-hand needle), k6, yo, k2tog, k9, sl m, k2, yo, sl 1, k2tog, psso, yo, *k3, yo, sl 1, k2tog, psso, yo; rep from * to 2 sts before m, k2, sl m, k10, yo, k2tog, k11—126 (132, 138, 144, 150, 156) sts rem.

ROW 8: Slide a bead up to start of work, BO 5 sts (1 st on right-hand needle), k6 yo, k2tog, k9, sl m, p6, *bead 1, p5; rep from * to 1 st before m, p1, sl m, k10, yo, k2tog, k6—121 (127, 133, 139, 145, 151) sts rem.

Rep these 8 rows 10 (10, 10, 12, 12, 12) more times, then work Rows 1–7 once more—126 (132, 138, 144, 150, 156) sts rem; piece measures about 12½ (12½, 12½, 14½, 14½)" (31.5 [31.5, 31.5, 37, 37] cm) from CO.

Edging

Change to smaller needles.

ROW 1: (WS) Slide a bead up to start of work, BO 5 sts (1 st on right-hand needle), k17, sl m, knit to next m, sl m, k18—121 (127, 133, 139, 145, 151) sts rem.

ROW 2: (RS) Knit.

BEAD ROW: (WS) K18, remove m, [p1, bead 1] 42 (45, 48, 51, 54, 57) times, p1, remove m, k18.

Work 2 rows in garter st, ending with a WS row. With RS facing, BO 21 sts, then work beaded picot BO as folls: *slip st from right-hand needle onto left-hand needle, use the cable method to CO 2 sts, bead 1, BO 5 sts; rep from * 27 (29, 31, 33, 35, 37) more times, BO rem 19 sts.

Finishing

Weave in loose ends. Block to finished measurements, being careful not to damage beads.

Assembly

Fold shrug in half lengthwise. With yarn threaded on a tapestry needle and using a mattress stitch or backstitch (see Glossary), sew garter-st edges tog.

added elements

A variety of techniques, such as fringe, appliqué, pom-poms, knitted rosettes, buttons, feathers, sequins, and ribbons, transform the knitted "blank canvases" of the projects in this chapter. Matilda (page 70), a simple drawstring purse, is covered with knitted rosettes. Ribbons threaded through an eyelet pattern create the shaping detail in the two versions of the Esme vest (page 74)—one with an Empire silhouette and the other with a 1940s-inspired nipped-in waist. Ella (page 80), an elegant lace scarf, is embellished with mother-of-pearl buttons. Cut velvet appliqué flowers and butterflies are sewn onto the decreasing panels of the otherwise simple Gracie vest (page 84). Fringe swishes around the hem of the cabled wrap, Tabatha (page 88), and three knitted rosettes form a chic corsage on the Amelia (page 92) cardigan.

FINISHED SIZE
About 7½" (19 cm) wide and 8¾"
(22 cm) long.

YARN
DK weight (#3 Light).

SHOWN HERE: Louisa Harding
Grace Wool and Silk (50% merino,
50% silk; 110 yd [101 m]/50 g): #28
Winter Berry, 3 balls.

NEEDLES
Sides: size U.S. 6 (4 mm).

Edging: size U.S. 5 (3.75 mm).

Flowers: size U.S. 7 (4.5 mm).

*Adjust needle size if necessary to
obtain the correct gauge.*

NOTIONS
Tapestry needle; beading needle;
felt fabric measuring 6" (15 cm)
square for bag base; felt fabric
measuring 17" (43 cm) wide and
8½" (21.5 cm) long for lining; 64
size 6° beads; sharp-point sewing
needle; matching thread.

GAUGE
22 stitches and 30 rows = 4"
(10 cm) in eyelet pattern on
medium-sized needles.

Matilda

This little purse reminds me of the drawstring purses that were
carried by the flapper girls of the 1920s. It provides a base for
lots of creative embellishment. The knitted flowers could be
made in an assortment of colors and yarns, depending on what
you have on hand. The large eyelets in the knitted fabric double
as flower centers and allow the colorful lining to peek through.
Although a bit labor-intensive, this flowered bag would make a
fabulous gift.

Purse

Lace Band

With smallest needles, CO 113 sts.

ROW 1: (RS) K1, *k5, sl 1, k2tog, psso, k6; rep from *—97 sts rem.

ROW 2: (WS) Knit.

ROW 3: K1, *k4, sl 1, k2tog, psso, k5; rep from *—81 sts rem.

ROW 4: Knit.

Change to medium-sized needles and work Rows 1–8 of Lace chart. Work 3 rows even in garter st (knit every row).

EYELET ROW: (WS) P1, *yo, p2tog; rep from *. Work 3 rows even in garter st.

INC ROW: (WS) K1, M1 (see Glossary), knit to end—82 sts; piece measures about 2½" (6.5 cm) from CO.

Work Rows 1–20 of Eyelet chart 2 times, then work Rows 1–6 once again—piece measures about 8¾" (22 cm) from CO.

Base

Change to smallest needles. Work 4 rows even in garter st.

DEC ROW 1: (RS) K1, *k8, k2tog; rep from * to last st, k1—74 sts rem.

Work 3 rows even in garter st.

DEC ROW 2: K1, *k7, k2tog; rep from * to last st, k1—66 sts rem.

Work 3 rows even in garter st.

DEC ROW 3: K1, *k6, k2tog; rep from * to last st, k1—58 sts rem.

Work 3 rows even in garter st.

DEC ROW 4: K1, *k5, k2tog; rep from * to last st, k1—50 sts rem.

Knit 1 row.

LACE CHART

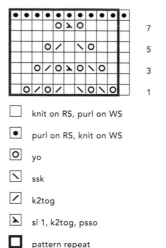

- ☐ knit on RS, purl on WS
- ⊡ purl on RS, knit on WS
- ⊙ yo
- ⟍ ssk
- ⟋ k2tog
- ⊼ sl 1, k2tog, psso
- ☐ pattern repeat

EYELET CHART

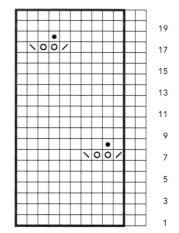

DEC ROW 5: K1, *k4, k2tog; rep from * to last st, k1—42 sts rem.

Knit 1 row.

DEC ROW 6: K1, *k3, k2tog; rep from * to last st, k1—34 sts rem.

Knit 1 row.

DEC ROW 7: K1, *k2, k2tog; rep from * to last st, k1—26 sts rem.

Knit 1 row.

DEC ROW 8: K1, *k1, k2tog; rep from * to last st, k1—18 sts rem.

Knit 1 row.

DEC ROW 9: K1, *k2tog; rep from * to last st, k1—10 sts rem.

Break off yarn, run yarn through rem sts, draw up, and fasten off.

Finishing

Weave in loose ends. Block to finished measurements.

Flowers (make 36)

With largest needles, CO 30 sts.

ROW 1: *K1, BO 3 sts (2 sts on right needle); rep from *—12 sts rem.

Cut yarn leaving a 10" (25.5 cm) tail. Thread tail through rem sts, pull to make a ⅜" (1 cm) hole in center, and fasten off. With yarn threaded on a tapestry needle, sew flowers to RS of purse, aligning the eyelets with the centers of the flowers and maintaining the center holes.

Lining

Cut the square base felt into a 6" (15 cm) diameter circle. Fold the lining felt in half with RS tog. With sharp-point sewing needle and matching thread, use a backstitch (see Glossary) with a ½" (1.3 cm) seam allowance to sew side seams. Sew circular base to lining. With WS tog, insert lining into purse. Turn under ½" (1.3 cm) of lining at top edge, and sew in place just below eyelet band.

Cord (make 2)

Cut four 5-foot (1.5 meter) lengths of yarn. Tie the lengths tog at each end with an overhand knot. Attach one end to a hook or door handle. Insert a knitting needle through the other end, then twist the needle to twist the yarn until it kinks on itself (the more twists, the firmer the finished cord). Hold the center of the cord in one hand (you may need some help), bring the ends tog, then allow them to untwist against each other. Tie the ends tog and trim—cord should measure about 19¾" (50 cm) long.

Starting at opposite sides of purse, thread twisted cord (substitute ribbon if you prefer) in and out of eyelet holes around top of purse. Trim ends. Thread each end through a flower and sew in place just above the knot. Thread 2 beads onto each end of yarn left for tassel, knot end of yarn, and trim.

FINISHED SIZE

About 36 (38, 40½, 42½, 44½, 47)" (91.5 [96.5, 103, 108, 113, 119.5] cm) bust circumference. Vests shown measure 38" (96.5 cm).

YARN

DK weight (#3 Light).

SHOWN HERE: *Striped version:* Louisa Harding Kashmir DK (55% wool, 10% cashmere, 35% microfiber; 116 yd [106 m]/50 g): #30 Hug (brown; A), 4 (5, 5, 6, 6, 7) balls; #31 Rust (B), 2 (2, 2, 2, 2, 3) balls; #32 Hot Pink (C), 2 (2, 2, 2, 2, 2) balls.

Solid version: Louisa Harding Jasmine (48% cotton, 39% bamboo, 10% silk, 3% polyester; 107 yd [98 m]/50 g): #24 Souk (burgundy), 6 (6, 7, 7, 8, 8) balls.

NEEDLES

Body: size U.S. 6 (4 mm).

Edging: size U.S. 3 (3.25 mm).

Adjust needle size if necessary to obtain the correct gauge.

NOTIONS

Tapestry needle; 79" (2 m) of ¼" (6 mm) ribbon.

GAUGE

22 sts and 30 rows = 4" (10 cm) in St st on larger needles.

Esme

Ribbons threaded through a striped eyelet pattern provide the shaping detail in this little vest. I've provided two distinct looks for this vest; one features stripes that highlight the very pretty edging and a contrasting ribbon that accentuates the waist shaping. The other (page 77) is worked in a single color that emphasizes the eyelet stripe pattern and a complementary satin ribbon tied in a cute bow at the front.

Striped version.

Back

With smaller needles and C (for striped version only), CO 163 (173, 183, 193, 203, 213) sts. Knit 1 RS row.

DEC ROW: (WS) K3, BO 6 sts (4 sts on right-hand needle), k3 (7 sts on right-hand needle), BO 6 sts (8 sts on right-hand needle), *k3, BO 6 sts, rep from * to last 3 sts, k3—67 (71, 75, 79, 83, 87) sts rem; 4 live sts bet each set of BO sts.

INC ROW: (RS) *K4, [yo] 2 times; rep from * to last 3 sts, k3—99 (105, 111, 117, 123, 129) sts.

NEXT ROW: K3, *(k1, p1) in double yo from previous row, k4, rep from *.

Work 2 rows in garter st (knit every row), ending with a WS row.

Work in eyelet patt (shown on charts on page 77) as foll, changing colors for striped version only:

ROWS 1 AND 2: With B, knit.

ROW 3: (RS) With C, knit.

ROW 4: (WS; eyelet row) With C, k1, p1, *yo, p2tog; rep from * to last st, k1.

ROWS 5 AND 6: With B, knit.

ROWS 7–20: With A, work in St st (knit RS rows; purl WS rows).

Rep Rows 1–20 until piece measures 14 (14, 14½, 14½, 15¼, 15¼)" (35.5 [35.5, 37, 37, 38.5, 38.5] cm) from CO, ending with WS row.

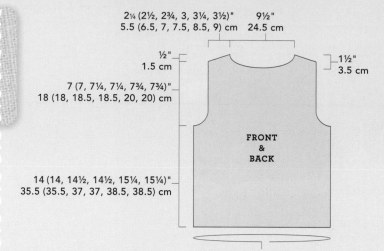

2¼ (2½, 2¾, 3, 3¼, 3½)"
5.5 (6.5, 7, 7.5, 8.5, 9) cm

9½"
24.5 cm

½"
1.5 cm

1½"
3.5 cm

7 (7, 7¼, 7¼, 7¾, 7¾)"
18 (18, 18.5, 18.5, 20, 20) cm

FRONT
&
BACK

14 (14, 14½, 14½, 15¼, 15¼)"
35.5 (35.5, 37, 37, 38.5, 38.5) cm

36 (38, 40½, 42½, 44½, 47)"
91 (97, 103, 108, 114, 119) cm

STRIPED EYELET CHART

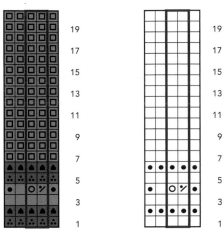

SOLID EYELET CHART

19
17
15
13
11
9
7
5
3
1

19
17
15
13
11
9
7
5
3
1

⊡	With A, knit on RS, purl on WS
⬞	With B, knit on RS, purl on WS
◆	With B, purl on RS, knit on WS
▨	With C, work in specified stitch
☐	knit on RS, purl on WS
•	purl on RS, knit on WS
O	yo
⟋	p2tog
⬜	pattern repeat

Solid version.

Shape Armholes

BO 4 (5, 5, 6, 6, 6) sts at beg of next 2 rows, then BO 4 (4, 5, 5, 5, 6) sts at beg of 2 foll rows—83 (87, 91, 95, 101, 105) sts rem.

DEC ROW: (RS) K3, k2tog, knit to last 5 sts, ssk, k3—2 sts dec'd.

Work 1 WS row even. Rep the last 2 rows 2 (2, 3, 4, 5, 5) more times—77 (81, 83, 85, 89, 93) sts rem. Work even in patt until armholes measure 6 (6, 6¼, 6¼, 6¾, 6¾)" (15 [15, 16, 16, 17, 17] cm), ending with a WS row.

Shape Shoulders and Neck

Right Shoulder

With RS facing, k18 (20, 21, 22, 24, 26), turn work—18 (20, 21, 22, 24, 26) right shoulder sts; rem sts will be worked later for neck and left shoulder.

NEXT ROW: (WS) P2tog, work as established to end of row—1 st dec'd.

NEXT ROW: (RS) Work as established to last last 2 sts, k2tog—1 st dec'd.

Rep the last 2 rows 2 more times—12 (14, 15, 16, 18, 20) sts rem. Work 1 WS row even. At armhole edge (beg of RS rows) BO 6 (7, 7, 8, 9, 10) sts once, then BO rem 6 (7, 8, 8, 9, 10) sts.

Left Shoulder

With RS facing, sl center 41 sts onto a holder for neck, rejoin appropriate yarn to rem sts, work in patt to end—18 (20, 21, 22, 24, 26) left shoulder sts.

NEXT ROW: (WS) Work as established to last 2 sts, ssp (see Glossary)—1 st dec'd.

NEXT ROW: (RS) Ssk, work as established to end of row—1 st dec'd.

Rep the last 2 rows 2 more times—12 (14, 15, 16, 18, 20) sts rem. Work 2 rows even, ending with a RS row. At armhole edge (beg of WS rows), BO 6 (7, 7, 8, 9, 10) sts once, then BO rem 6 (7, 8, 8, 9, 10) sts.

Front

CO and work as for back.

Finishing

Block pieces to finished measurements. With yarn threaded on a tapestry needle, sew front to back at one shoulder. Weave in loose ends.

Neck Edging

With B (for striped version only), smaller needles, RS facing, and beg at unseamed shoulder, pick up and knit 10 sts along neck edge, k41 held neck sts, pick up and knit 10 sts to shoulder seam and 9 sts along neck edge, k41 held neck sts, pick up and knit 10 sts along neck to shoulder—121 sts total. Knit 1 (WS) row. Change to C (for striped version only) and knit 1 row.

EYELET ROW: (WS) K1, p1, *yo, p2tog; rep from * to last st, k1.

Change to B and work 3 rows in garter st, ending with a RS row. With WS facing, BO all sts knitwise.

With yarn threaded on a tapestry needle, sew left shoulder and neck edging seam.

Armhole Edging

With A (for striped version only), smaller needle, and RS facing, pick up and knit 46 (46, 50, 50, 54, 54) sts evenly spaced to shoulder seam and 46 (46, 50, 50, 54, 54) sts to side seam—92 (92, 100, 100, 108, 108) sts total. Knit 2 rows. With WS facing, BO all sts knitwise. With yarn threaded on a tapestry needle, sew armhole edging and side seams.

Embellishment

Choose the row of eyelets to add ribbon—under the bust for empire styling or at the waist for waist definition. Beg and end at center front, thread ribbon through eyelets as shown in photograph. Tie ends into a bow to secure.

FINISHED SIZE

Hulda Scarf: About 10½" (26.5 cm) wide and 55½" (141 cm) long.

Grace Hand-Dyed Scarf: About 9¾" (25 cm) wide and 44½" (113 cm) long.

YARN

Hulda version: Chunky (#5 Bulky).

Grace Hand-Dyed version: Worsted Weight (#4 Medium).

SHOWN HERE: *Hulda version:* Louisa Harding Hulda (50% wool, 30% acrylic, 20% linen; 110 yd [101 m]/50 g): #14 Russett, 3 balls.

Grace Hand-Dyed version: Louisa Harding Grace Hand Dyed (50% merino, 50% silk; 110 yd [101 m]/ 50 g):#20 Crackle, 3 hanks.

NEEDLES

Hulda version: size U.S. 10 (6 mm).

Grace Hand-Dyed version: size U.S. 8 (5 mm).

Adjust needle size if necessary to obtain the correct gauge.

NOTIONS

Tapestry needle; forty-eight ¼" (6 mm) and sixteen ⅞" (2.2 cm) mother-of-pearl buttons for Hulda Scarf; thirty-eight ¼" (6 mm) mother-of-pearl buttons for Grace Hand-Dyed Scarf; sharp-point sewing needle; matching sewing thread.

GAUGE

Hulda version: 15 stitches and 19 rows = 4" (10 cm) in lace pattern on size U.S. 10 (6 mm) needles.

Grace Hand-Dyed version: 16 stitches and 28 rows = 4" (10 cm) in lace pattern on size U.S. 8 (5 mm) needles.

Ella

I enjoy combining stitch patterns that complement one another in an overall design. This scarf includes an undulating edge, a small lace repeat worked alongside a large lace panel, and a few eyelets thrown in for good measure. The two variations shown here are worked on the same number of stitches but with two different yarns to produce two different sizes. Both scarves are embellished with mother-of-pearl buttons; one highlights the pattern repeats, the other accents the undulating edge.

Grace Hand-Dyed version.

Scarf

Work picot CO as folls: *Use the cable method (see Glossary) to CO 5 sts, BO 2 sts, slip st on right-hand needle back onto left-hand needle (3 sts on left-hand needle); rep from * until there are 39 sts on needle. Work 4 rows in garter st (knit every row). Work Rows 1–16 of Lace and Edging chart 16 times for Hulda Scarf and 19 times for Grace Hand-Dyed scarf. Work 3 rows in garter st. Work picot BO as foll: BO 3 sts, *slip st on right-hand needle back onto left-hand needle, use the cable method CO 2 sts, then BO 5 sts, rep from * to end.

Finishing

Block to finished measurements. Weave in loose ends.

Hulda version.

□	knit on RS, purl on WS
•	purl on RS, knit on WS
O	yo
∕	k2tog
＼	ssk
⋋	sl 1, k2tog, psso
■	no stitch
⌒	BO

for Hulda Scarf only:

▨	small button placement
▨	large button placement

LACE AND EDGING CHART

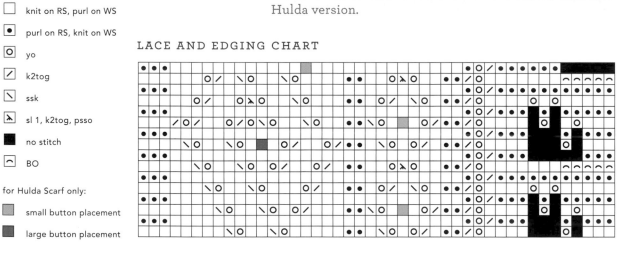

Embellishment

Hulda Scarf

With matching thread, sharp-point sewing needle, and using the chart as a guide, sew small buttons to the center of each large patt rep and to the center of each small patt rep at the right edge of scarf. Sew large buttons along Row 16 of large patt rep.

Grace Hand-Dyed Scarf

Using the photograph as a guide, sew a button to each point along the right-hand side edge.

FINISHED SIZE
About 37 (41, 45)" (94 [104,
114.5] cm) bust circumference with
2" to 4" (5 to 10 cm) ease. Vest
shown measures 37" (94 cm).

YARN
Worsted weight (#4 Medium).

SHOWN HERE: Louisa Harding
Kashmir Aran (55% wool, 10% cashmere, 35% microfiber; 83 yd
[76 m]/50 g): #35 Ember (burgundy),
12 (14, 16) balls.

NEEDLES
Body: size U.S. 8 (5 mm).

Edging: size U.S. 7 (4.5 mm).

*Adjust needle size if necessary to
obtain the correct gauge.*

NOTIONS
Tapestry needle; a selection of velvet flowers for appliqué (available
online from a variety of sources);
sharp-point sewing needle; matching thread.

GAUGE
18 sts and 27 rows = 4" (10 cm)
in panel stitch pattern on larger
needles.

Gracie

To decorate the shaped panels in this A-line design, I added
cut velvet appliqués that I purchased at La Droguerie, a lovely
shop in Paris. Worked in the traditional method, the velvet is
stiffened with starch, and the shapes are created by applying
a heavy lead stamp that adds texture as it cuts out the shapes.
Look for similar appliqués at craft, antique, and thrift stores.

Back

With smaller needle, work picot CO as folls:
*Use the cable method (see Glossary) to CO 5
sts, BO 2 sts, sl st from right-hand needle onto
left-hand needle (3 sts on left-hand needle);
rep from * until there are 171 (192, 210) sts on
needle, CO 2 (0, 1) more st(s)—173 (192, 211)
sts. Work 4 rows in garter st (knit every row),
ending with a WS row. Change to larger needle
and work panel patt as foll:

ROW 1: (RS) K9, [k1, yo, k2tog, k16] 8 (9, 10)
times, k1, yo, k2tog, k9.

ROW 2: K1, p8, [k1, yo, k2tog, p16] 8 (9, 10)
times, k1, yo, k2tog, p8, k1.

Rep these 2 rows 14 more times, ending with
a WS row—piece measures about 5" (12.5 cm)
from CO.

DEC ROW 1: (RS) K7, k2tog, [k1, yo, k2tog, ssk,
k12, k2tog] 8 (9, 10) times, k1, yo, k2tog, ssk,
k7—155 (172, 189) sts rem.

NEXT ROW: (WS) K1, p7, [k1, yo, k2tog, p14] 8
(9, 10) times, k1, yo, k2tog, p7, k1.

NEXT ROW: K8, [k1, yo, k2tog, k14] 8 (9, 10)
times, k1, yo, k2tog, k8.

Rep the last 2 rows 7 more times, then work the
WS row once more—piece measures about 7¾"
(19.5 cm) from CO.

DEC ROW 2: (RS) K6, k2tog, [k1, yo, k2tog, ssk,
k10, k2tog] 8 (9, 10) times, k1, yo, k2tog, ssk,
k6—137 (152, 167) sts rem.

NEXT ROW: (WS) K1, p6, [k1, yo, k2tog, p12] 8
(9, 10) times, k1, yo, k2tog, p6, k1.

NEXT ROW: K7, [k1, yo, k2tog, k12] 8 (9, 10)
times, k1, yo, k2tog, k7.

Rep the last 2 rows 7 more times, then work
the WS row once more—piece measures about
10¼" (26 cm) from CO.

DEC ROW 3: (RS) K5, k2tog, [k1, yo, k2tog, ssk,
k8, k2tog] 8 (9, 10) times, k1, yo, k2tog, ssk,
k5—119 (132, 145) sts rem.

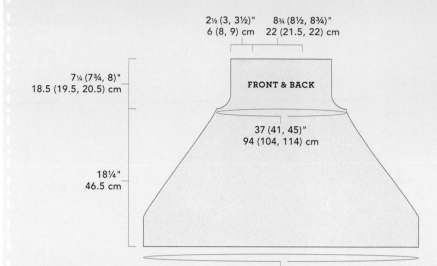

2½ (3, 3½)"
6 (8, 9) cm

8¾ (8½, 8¾)"
22 (21.5, 22) cm

7¼ (7¾, 8)"
18.5 (19.5, 20.5) cm

FRONT & BACK

37 (41, 45)"
94 (104, 114) cm

18¼"
46.5 cm

77 (85¼, 93¾)"
195.5 (216.5, 238) cm

NEXT ROW: K1, p5, [k1, yo, k2tog, p10] 8 (9, 10) times, k1, yo, k2tog, p5, k1.

NEXT ROW: K6, [k1, yo, k2tog, k10] 8 (9, 10) times, k1, yo, k2tog, k6.

Rep the last 2 rows 7 more times, then work the WS row once more—piece measures about 13" (33 cm) from CO.

DEC ROW 4: (RS) K4, k2tog, [k1, yo, k2tog, ssk, k6, k2tog] 8 (9, 10) times, k1, yo, k2tog, ssk, k4—101 (112, 123) sts rem.

NEXT ROW: K1, p4, [k1, yo, k2tog, p8] 8 (9, 10) times, k1, yo, k2tog, p4, k1.

NEXT ROW: K5, [k1, yo, k2tog, k8] 8 (9, 10) times, k1, yo, k2tog, k5.

Rep the last 2 rows 7 more times, then work the WS row once more—piece measures about 15½" (39.5 cm) from CO.

DEC ROW 5: (RS) K3, k2tog, [k1, yo, k2tog, ssk, k4, k2tog] 8 (9, 10) times, k1, yo, k2tog, ssk, k3—83 (92, 101) sts rem.

NEXT ROW: K1, p3, [k1, yo, k2tog, p6] 8 (9, 10) times, k1, yo, k2tog, p3, k1.

NEXT ROW: K4, [k1, yo, k2tog, k6] 8 (9, 10) times, k1, yo, k2tog, k4.

Rep the last 2 rows 7 more times, then work the WS row once more—piece measures about 18¼" (46.5 cm) from CO.

Shape Armholes

Keeping in patt, BO 4 (4, 6) sts at beg of next 2 rows, then BO 3 (4, 4) sts at beg of foll 2 rows—69 (76, 81) sts rem.

DEC ROW: (RS) K2tog, work in patt to last 2 sts, ssk—2 sts dec'd.

Work 1 WS row even. Rep the last 2 rows 3 (4, 4) more times—61 (66, 71) sts rem. Work even in patt until armholes measure 6¼ (6¾, 7)" (16 [17, 18] cm), ending with a WS row. Change to smaller needles. Work 5 rows even in garter st.

EYELET ROW: (WS) P2, *yo, p2tog; rep from * to last 1 (2, 1) st(s), p1 (2, 1).

Work 3 rows in garter st, ending with a RS row. With WS facing, use the picot method to BO as foll: BO 11 (14, 16) sts, *sl st on right-hand needle back onto left-hand needle, use the backward-loop method (see Glossary) to CO 2 sts, BO 5 sts; rep from * 14 more times, BO rem 8 (10, 13) sts.

Front

CO and work as for back.

Finishing

Block pieces to finished measurements. With yarn threaded on a tapestry needle, sew front to back at shoulders, leaving center picot edging sts open for neck. Weave in loose ends.

Armhole Edging

With smaller needles and RS facing, pick up and knit 37 (40, 43) sts evenly spaced to shoulder seam and 37 (40, 43) sts evenly spaced to side seam—74 (80, 86) sts total. Work 2 rows in garter st. With WS facing, BO all sts knitwise. With yarn threaded on a tapestry needle, sew armhole edging and side seams.

Embellishment

Pin each velvet appliqué as desired. With sharp-point sewing needle and matching thread, use whipstitches (see Glossary) to secure the entire perimeter of each appliqué.

FINISHED SIZE
About 47" (119.5 cm) circumference at hem, 30" (76 cm) circumference at shoulder, and 13¾" (35 cm) long, excluding fringe.

YARN
Worsted weight (#4 Medium).

SHOWN HERE: Louisa Harding Thistle (60% merino, 40% suri alpaca; 98 yd [90 m]/50 g): #9 Ginger, 5 balls.

NEEDLES
Size U.S. 8 (5 mm): straight and 24" (60 cm) circular (cir).

Adjust needle size if necessary to obtain the correct gauge.

NOTIONS
Cable needle (cn); marker (m); tapestry needle; size G/6 (4.5 mm) crochet hook.

GAUGE
16 stitches and 24 rows = 4" (10 cm) in garter stitch for cable edging; 18-st repeat at lower edge of yoke measures 3½" (9 cm) wide.

Tabitha

A large chunky cable creates a visual statement at the edging of this cabled cape and provides a nice base on which to attach fringe. Because fringe creates the illusion of adding length, it is a great way to disguise a project that is a little too short. Adding beads to the fringe for extra weight and drape or work the fringe in a contrasting color or fiber to add color and texture.

Stitch Guide

10/10RC

Sl 10 sts onto cn and hold in back, k10, k10 from cn.

3/3LC

Sl 3 sts onto cn and hold in front; k3, k3 from cn.

3/3RC

Sl 3 sts onto cn and hold in back, k3, k3 from cn.

2/2LC

Sl 2 sts onto cn and hold in front, k2, k2 from cn.

2/2RC

Sl 2 sts onto cn and hold in back, k2, k2 from cn.

1/1LC

Sl 1 st onto cn and hold in front, k1, k1 from cn.

1/1RC

Sl 1 st onto cn and hold in back, k1, k1 from cn.

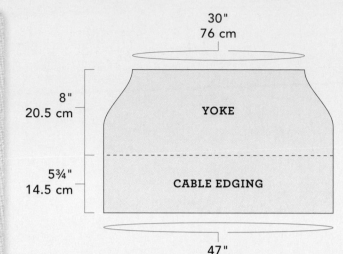

Cape

Cable Edging

With straight needles, CO 24 sts. Beg with a RS row, work 2 rows in St st (knit RS rows; purl WS rows).

INC ROW: (RS) K4, yo, k2tog, k6, [M1 (see Glossary), k2] 6 times—30 sts.

NEXT ROW: K1, p8, k2, p8, k6, yo, k2tog, k3.

Work Rows 1–24 of Cable Edging chart 11 times, then work Rows 1–18 once more—piece measures about 47" (119.5 cm) from CO.

CABLE EDGING CHART

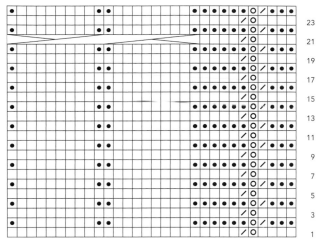

YOKE CHART

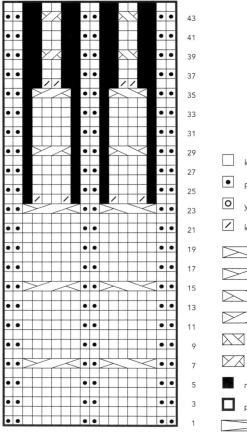

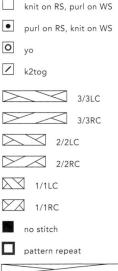

	knit on RS, purl on WS
•	purl on RS, knit on WS
O	yo
/	k2tog
	3/3LC
	3/3RC
	2/2LC
	2/2RC
	1/1LC
	1/1RC
■	no stitch
□	pattern repeat

10/10RC

DEC ROW: (RS) K4, yo, k2tog, k6, [k2tog, k1] 6 times—24 sts rem.

Purl 1 WS row. With RS facing, BO all sts.

With yarn threaded on a tapestry needle, use a mattress st (see Glossary) to join CO and BO edges tog to form a ring, being careful not to twist into a helix.

Yoke

Turn edging 45 degrees counterclockwise so that the straight garter-st edge is at the top of the work.

With cir needle, RS facing, and starting at seam of edging ring, pick up and knit 216 sts evenly spaced around straight edge of ring. Place marker (pm) and join for working in rnds. Work Rnds 1–44 of Yoke chart—120 sts rem; piece measures about 7¾" (19.5 cm) from pick-up rnd.

Purl 1 rnd, then knit 1 rnd. Turn work and with WS facing, BO all sts kwise.

Finishing

Weave in loose ends. Block to finished measurements.

Fringe

Cut 160 lengths of yarn, each about 9" (23 cm) long. To attach fringe, fold one length in half and use a crochet hook to draw the fold end through the edge st of the cable edging, pull the loose ends through the loop, and pull firmly to secure. Rep for the rem lengths, spacing them evenly around the cable edge.

FINISHED SIZE
About 32¾ (34¾, 37, 39, 41½, 43½)" (83 [88.5, 94, 99, 105.5, 110.5] cm) bust circumference, allowing about 1" to 2" (2.5 to 5 cm) of ease. Sweater shown measures 32¾" (83 cm).

YARN
Chunky weight (#5 Bulky).

SHOWN HERE: Louisa Harding Rossetti (67% merino wool, 28% silk, 5% polyamide; 76 yd [70 m]/50 g): #5 Ember, 7 (8, 8, 9, 9, 10) balls.

NEEDLES
Body and sleeves: size U.S. 10 (6 mm). Edging: size U.S. 8 (5 mm).

Adjust needle size if necessary to obtain the correct gauge.

NOTIONS
Tapestry needle; nine ½" (1.3 cm) and three ¾" (2 cm) mother-of-pearl buttons.

GAUGE
15 stitches and 20 rows = 4" (10 cm) in St st on larger needles.

Amelia

This delicate cardigan is reminiscent of those that 1940s film stars draped around their shoulders to keep cool evening breezes at bay. A bouquet of knitted rosettes at the left front neck, secured by large mother-of-pearl buttons, provides a chic corsage that is forever fresh. The front is closed with buttons that fasten through discreet loops worked as part of the edging bind-off.

Back

With smaller needles, CO 51 (55, 59, 63, 67, 71) sts. Work 4 rows in garter st (knit every row). Change to larger needles. Beg with a RS row, work 8 rows in St st (knit RS rows; purl WS rows).

INC ROW: (RS) K3, M1 (see Glossary), knit to last 3 sts, M1, k3—2 sts inc'd.

Work 7 rows even in St st. Rep the last 8 rows 3 more times—59 (63, 67, 71, 75, 79) sts. Work even until piece measures 11 (11, 11½, 11½, 12¼, 12¼)" (28 [28, 29, 29, 31, 31] cm from CO, ending with a WS row.

Shape Armholes

BO 3 (4, 4, 5, 5, 6) sts at beg of next 2 rows, then BO 2 (2, 3, 3, 3, 3) sts at beg of foll 2 rows—49 (51, 53, 55, 59, 61) sts rem.

DEC ROW: (RS) K3, k2tog, knit to last 5 sts, ssk, k3—2 sts dec'd.

Purl 1 WS row. Rep the last 2 rows 1 (1, 2, 2, 3, 3) more time(s)—45 (47, 47, 49, 51, 53) sts rem. Work even in St st until armholes measure 7 (7, 7½, 7½, 8, 8)" (18 [18, 19, 19, 20.5, 20.5] cm), ending with a WS row.

Shape Shoulders and Neck

BO 4 (4, 4, 5, 5) sts at beg of next 2 rows—37 (39, 39, 41, 41, 43) sts rem.

NEXT ROW: (RS) BO 4 (4, 4, 4, 5, 5) sts, knit until there are 6 (7, 7, 8, 7, 8) sts on right-hand needle, turn work—rem 27 (28, 28, 29, 29, 30) sts will be worked later.

Right Shoulder

Working 6 (7, 7, 8, 7, 8) right shoulder sts only, with WS facing, BO 3 sts, purl to end—3 (4, 4, 5, 4, 5) sts rem. BO all sts.

Left Shoulder

With RS facing, rejoin yarn to 27 (28, 28, 29, 29, 30) live sts, BO center 17 sts for back neck, knit to end—10 (11, 11, 12, 12, 13) sts rem.

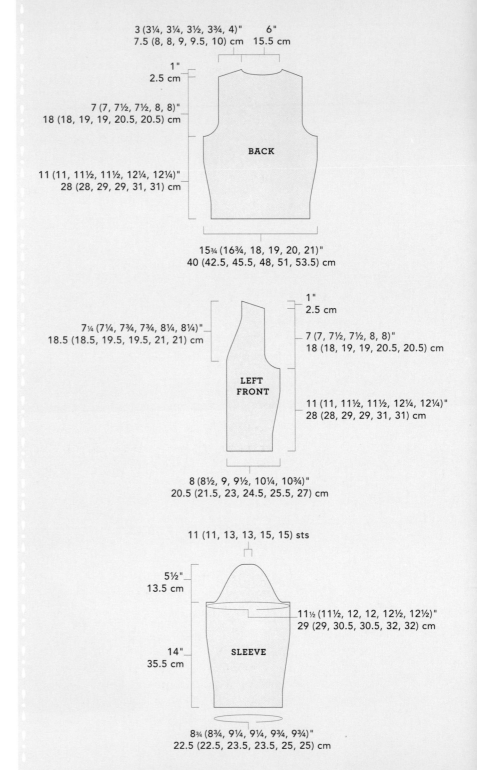

3 (3¼, 3¼, 3½, 3¾, 4)"
7.5 (8, 8, 9, 9.5, 10) cm   6" 15.5 cm

1" 2.5 cm

7 (7, 7½, 7½, 8, 8)"
18 (18, 19, 19, 20.5, 20.5) cm

BACK

11 (11, 11½, 11½, 12¼, 12¼)"
28 (28, 29, 29, 31, 31) cm

15¾ (16¾, 18, 19, 20, 21)"
40 (42.5, 45.5, 48, 51, 53.5) cm

1" 2.5 cm

7¼ (7¼, 7¾, 7¾, 8¼, 8¼)"
18.5 (18.5, 19.5, 19.5, 21, 21) cm

7 (7, 7½, 7½, 8, 8)"
18 (18, 19, 19, 20.5, 20.5) cm

LEFT FRONT

11 (11, 11½, 11½, 12¼, 12¼)"
28 (28, 29, 29, 31, 31) cm

8 (8½, 9, 9½, 10¼, 10¾)"
20.5 (21.5, 23, 24.5, 25.5, 27) cm

11 (11, 13, 13, 15, 15) sts

5½" 13.5 cm

11½ (11½, 12, 12, 12½, 12½)"
29 (29, 30.5, 30.5, 32, 32) cm

14" 35.5 cm

SLEEVE

8¾ (8¾, 9¼, 9¼, 9¾, 9¾)"
22.5 (22.5, 23.5, 23.5, 25, 25) cm

NEXT ROW: (WS) BO 4 (4, 4, 4, 5, 5) sts, purl to end—6 (7, 7, 8, 7, 8) sts rem. At beg of next RS row, BO 3 sts, knit to end—3 (4, 4, 5, 4, 5) sts rem. BO rem sts.

Left Front

With smaller needles, CO 26 (28, 30, 32, 34, 36) sts. Work 4 rows in garter st. Change to larger needles. Beg with a RS row, work 8 rows in St st.

INC ROW: (RS) K3, M1, knit to end—1 st inc'd.

Work 7 rows even in St st. Rep the last 8 rows 3 more times—30 (32, 34, 36, 38, 40) sts. Work even until piece measures 11 (11, 11½, 11½, 12¼, 12¼)" (28 [28, 29, 29, 31, 31] cm) from CO, ending with a WS row.

Shape Armhole and Neck

At armhole edge (beg of RS rows), BO 3 (4, 4, 5, 5, 6) sts once, then BO 2 (2, 3, 3, 3, 3) sts once—25 (26, 27, 28, 30, 31) sts rem. Work 1 WS row even.

DEC ROW: (RS) K3, k2tog, knit to last 5 sts, ssk, k3—2 sts dec'd.

Purl 1 WS row. Rep the last 2 rows 1 (1, 2, 2, 3, 3) more time(s)—21 (22, 21, 22, 22, 23) sts rem.

NEXT ROW: (RS) Knit to last 5 sts, ssk, k3—1 st dec'd.

Purl 1 WS row. Rep the last 2 rows 9 (9, 8, 8, 7, 7) more times—11 (12, 12, 13, 14, 15) sts rem. Work even until armhole measures 7 (7, 7½, 7½, 8, 8)" (18 [18, 19, 19, 20, 20] cm), ending with a WS row.

Shape Shoulder

At armhole edge (beg of RS rows), BO 4 (4, 4, 4, 5, 5) sts 2 times, then BO rem 3 (4, 4, 5, 4, 5) sts.

Right Front

With smaller needles, CO 26 (28, 30, 32, 34, 36) sts. Work 4 rows in garter st. Change to larger needles. Beg with a RS row, work 8 rows in St st.

INC ROW: (RS) Knit to last 3 sts, M1, k3—1 st inc'd.

Work 7 rows even in St st. Rep the last 8 rows 3 more times—30 (32, 34, 36, 38, 40) sts. Work even until piece measures 11 (11, 11½, 11½, 12¼, 12¼)" (28 [28, 29, 29, 31, 31] cm) from CO, ending with a RS row.

Shape Armhole and Neck

At armhole edge (beg of WS rows), BO 3 (4, 4, 5, 5, 6) sts once, then BO 2 (2, 3, 3, 3, 3) sts once—25 (26, 27, 28, 30, 31) sts rem.

DEC ROW: (RS) K3, k2tog, knit to last 5 sts, ssk, k3—2 sts dec'd.

Purl 1 WS row. Rep the last 2 rows 1 (1, 2, 2, 3, 3) more time(s)—21 (22, 21, 22, 22, 23) sts rem.

NEXT ROW: (RS) K3, k2tog, knit to end—1 st dec'd.

Purl 1 WS row. Rep the last 2 rows 9 (9, 8, 8, 7, 7) more times—11 (12, 12, 13, 14, 15) sts rem. Work even until armhole measures 7 (7, 7½, 7½, 8, 8)" (18 [18, 19, 19, 20.5, 20.5] cm), ending with a RS row.

Shape Shoulder

At armhole edge (beg of WS rows), BO 4 (4, 4, 4, 5, 5) sts 2 times, then BO rem 3 (4, 4, 5, 4, 5) sts.

Sleeves

With smaller needles, CO 33 (33, 35, 35, 37, 37) sts. Work 4 rows in garter st. Change to larger needles. Beg with a RS row, work 8 rows in St st.

INC ROW: (RS) K3, M1, knit to last 3 sts, M1, k3—2 sts inc'd.

Work 7 rows even in St st. Rep the last 8 rows 4 more times—43 (43, 45, 45, 47, 47) sts. Work even until piece measures 14" (35.5 cm) for all sizes, ending with a WS row.

Shape Cap

BO 4 sts at beg of next 2 rows—35 (35, 37, 37, 39, 39) sts rem.

NEXT ROW: (RS) K2tog, knit to last 2 sts, ssk—2 sts dec'd.

NEXT ROW: (WS) Ssp (see Glossary), purl to last 2 sts, p2tog—2 sts dec'd.

Rep RS dec row once more, then rep RS dec row every other row (purl WS rows) 2 more times—25 (25, 27, 27, 29, 29) sts rem. Dec 1 st each end of needle every 4th row 3 times, then every row 4 times—11 (11, 13, 13, 15, 15) sts rem. BO 3 sts at beg of next 2 rows—5 (5, 7, 7, 9, 9) sts rem. BO all sts.

Finishing

Block pieces to finished measurements. With yarn threaded on a tapestry needle, use a backstitch (see Glossary) to sew fronts to back at shoulders.

Buttonhole Band

With smaller needles, RS facing, and beg at lower right front edge, pick up and knit 44 (44, 47, 47, 50, 50) sts evenly spaced to start of front neck shaping, 32 (32, 35, 35, 38, 38) sts to shoulder seam, 24 sts across back neck to shoulder seam, 32 (32, 35, 35, 38, 38) sts along center left front edge to start of front neck shaping, and 44 (44, 47, 47, 50, 50) sts to CO edge—176 (176, 188, 188, 200) sts total. Work 2 rows in garter st, ending with a RS row. Change to larger needles.

BUTTONHOLE ROW: BO 132 (132, 141, 141, 150, 150) sts knitwise, *make a 4-chain button loop as foll: [insert left-hand needle into last st on right-hand needle and knit this st] 4 times, pick up last BO st with left-hand needle and knit this st again, then lift the last st of the chain over this st and off the needle, BO 4 sts; rep from * 8 more times, BO to end of row.

Rosettes *(make 3)*

With smaller needles, CO 112 sts. Work short-rows (see Glossary) as foll:

ROW 1: (RS) Knit.

ROW 2: (WS) K2, [k1, return this st to left-hand needle, pass the next 8 sts on left-hand needle over this st and off needle, knit the first st again, k2] 10 times—32 sts rem.

ROW 3: K24, wrap next st, turn work.

ROW 4: Knit to end.

ROW 5: K16, wrap next st, turn work.

ROW 6: Knit to end.

ROW 7: K8, wrap next st, turn work.

ROW 8: Knit to end.

Cut yarn, thread tail through sts on needle, pull tight to create a rosette, and secure with a few stitches. Pin rosettes as desired on left front of garment and sew in place with yarn threaded on a tapestry needle. Sew a large mother-of-pearl button in the center of each flower.

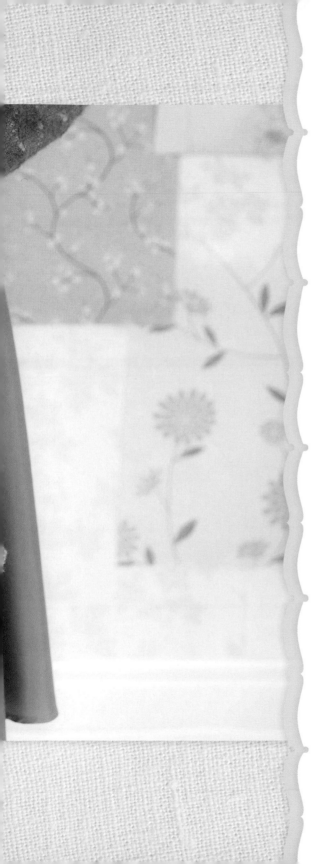

in the details

This chapter showcases projects that use combinations of the techniques that will capture your imagination and provide creative ideas for your own embellishment endeavors. Poppy (page 100), worked in two colorways, shows how different embellishments can transform a simple beanie. Madeleine (page 104), a large blanket-style shawl, makes use of duplicate-stitch lettering, knitted flowers, and appliqué. An allover beaded pattern with edge details gives an elegant look to the simple-to-knit Nina scarf (page 108). Ivy (page 112), a purse with a striped textured background, is made special with ribbons, rosettes, buttons, and pom-poms. Knitted flowers and blossom-shaped buttons add texture and interest to the elegant April bolero (page 118), which is topped off with a big ribbon bow. Marigold (page 124) uses the charms from a broken bracelet to add interest to a knitted ruffle edging.

YARN

Worsted weight (#4 Medium).

SHOWN HERE: Louisa Harding Thistle (60% merino, 40% suri alpaca; 98 yd [90 m]/50 g).

Striped version: #14 Lavender (A), #16 Surf (B), and #3 Stone (C), 1 ball each.

Two-color version: #8 Berry (A), 2 balls; #12 Winter (B), 1 ball.

NEEDLES

Hat: size U.S. 8 (5 mm).

Edging: size U.S. 6 (4 mm).

Adjust needle size if necessary to obtain the correct gauge.

NOTIONS

Tapestry needle; 39" (99 cm) of ⅜" (1 cm) ribbon. Striped version only: 26 size 6° clear silver-lined beads; twenty-six ½" (1.3 cm) flower-shaped sequins; oddments of yarn for knitted flowers; 1 antique beaded brooch (optional). Two-color version only: one 1¾" (4.5 cm) velvet flower and two 1¾" (4.5 cm) leaf appliqués; sharp-point sewing needle; matching thread.

GAUGE

18 stitches and 24 rows = 4" (10 cm) in stockinette stitch on larger needles.

Poppy

I've shown this simple beanie pattern two ways—one is knitted in subtle stripes (inspired by an antique brooch) and embellished with small flowers, sequins, and beads; the other is knitted in just two shades and embellished with a large rosette (page 103) for a stunning statement. A ribbon threaded through eyelets in the edging adds a pretty accent while preventing the hat from stretching. The embellishment possibilities are endless—be inspired by a found object or a gift from a loved one.

Striped version.

FINISHED SIZE
About 23" (58.5 cm) wide and
45½" (115.5 cm) long.

YARN
Worsted weight (#4 Medium).

SHOWN HERE: Louisa Harding
Grace Wool and Silk (50% merino,
50% silk; 110 yd [101 m]/50 g):
#24 Mallow (pink; A), #20 Whale
(gray; B), #21 Rosy (mauve; C), #22
Reflection (sky blue; D), #23 Sloe
(purple; E), and #25 Kiwi (green; F),
2 balls each.

NEEDLES
Edging and intarsia: size U.S. 7
(4.5 mm).

Picot CO: size U.S. 6 (4 mm).

*Adjust needle size if necessary to
obtain the correct gauge.*

NOTIONS
Tapestry needle; sharp-point sewing needle and matching thread;
assorted buttons; ½" (1.3 cm) velvet cut flower appliqués (available
from craft stores); assorted beads.

GAUGE
20 stitches and 28 rows = 4"
(10 cm) in stockinette stitch on
larger needles.

Madeleine

According to fashion designer Vivienne Westwood, the most
versatile garment is a strip of fabric that can be manipulated
into many different styles. This strip of intarsia fabric can be-
come a wrap, shawl, skirt, scarf, or blanket. To add weight and
provide a place to attach a shawl pin, I worked an edging along
with the intarsia squares. You can embellish this piece sparsely
or go over the top to record events and family occasions: buttons from a favorite worn-out dress, ribbons from presents, etc.

Shawl/Blanket

With F and smaller needles, work picot CO on as foll: Use the cable method (see Glossary) to CO 5 sts, BO 2 sts, sl st on right-hand needle onto left-hand needle (3 sts on left-hand needle); rep from * until there are 111 sts, use the cable method to CO 2 more sts—113 sts.

Work 4 rows even in garter st (knit every row).

Bottom Edging

Change to larger needles. Work Rows 1–12 of Bottom Edging Chart.

Work 3 rows even in garter st.

NEXT ROW: (WS) K2, p1, *yo, p2tog; rep from * to last 2 sts, k2.

Work 2 rows even in garter st, ending with a WS row—piece measures about 2¾" (7 cm) from CO.

Intarsia Section

Joining and cutting off colors as necessary, work side edging and intarsia (twisting yarns at color changes to prevent holes) as foll:

ROW 1: (RS) With F, k3, yo, k4, yo, k2tog, k1; join A and k31; join B and k31; join C and k31; join F, k2, yo, k2tog, k3, yo, k3—115 sts.

ROW 2: With F, k8, yo, k2tog, k1; with C p31, with B p31, with A p31, with F, k2, yo, k2tog, k7.

ROW 3: With F, k3, yo, k1, yo, k4, yo, k2tog, k1; with A k31, with B k31, with C k31; with F, k2, yo, k2tog, k3, yo, k1, yo, k3—119 sts.

ROW 4: With F, k10, yo, k2tog, k1; with C p31, with B p31, with A p31; with F, k2, yo, k2tog, k9.

ROW 5: With F, k5, yo, k1, yo, k4, yo, k2tog, k1; with A k31, with B k31, with C k31; with F, k2, yo, k2tog, k3, yo, k1, yo, k5—123 sts.

ROW 6: With F, k12, yo, k2tog, k1; with C p31, with B p31, with A p31; with F, k2, yo, k2tog, k11.

TOP EDGING CHART

BOTTOM EDGING CHART

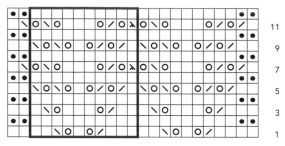

- ☐ knit on RS, purl on WS
- ● purl on RS, knit on WS
- ◯ yo
- ◹ ssk
- ◿ k2tog
- ⅄ sl 1, k2tog, psso
- ☐ pattern repeat

INTARSIA DIAGRAM

31 sts 40 rows A	31 sts 40 rows E	31 sts 40 rows D
31 sts 40 rows C	31 sts 40 rows B	31 sts 40 rows A
31 sts 40 rows E	31 sts 40 rows D	31 sts 40 rows C
31 sts 40 rows B	31 sts 40 rows A	31 sts 40 rows E
31 sts 40 rows D	31 sts 40 rows C	31 sts 40 rows B
31 sts 40 rows A	31 sts 40 rows E	31 sts 40 rows D
31 sts 40 rows C	31 sts 40 rows B	31 sts 40 rows A

ROW 7: With F, BO 5 sts (1 st on right-hand needle), k6, yo, k2tog, k1; with A k31, with B k31, with C k31; with F, k2, yo, k2tog, k11—118 sts rem.

ROW 8: With F, BO 5 sts, k6, yo, k2tog, k1; with C p31, with B p31, with A p31; with F, k2, yo, k2tog, k6—113 sts rem.

ROWS 9–280: Rep Rows 1–8 four more times in the same colors, then change colors according to Intarsia chart and work Rows 1–8 five times for each color block.

With F, work 3 rows even in garter st, ending with a RS row—piece measures about 42¾" (108.5 cm) from CO.

Top Edging

With WS facing, k2, p1, *yo, p2tog; rep from * to last 2 sts, k2.

Work 2 rows even in garter st, ending with a WS row. Work Rows 1–12 of Top Edging Chart.

Change to smaller needles and work 4 rows even in garter st. Work picot BO as foll: BO 3 sts, *sl st from right-hand needle onto left-hand needle, use the cable method to CO 2 sts, BO 5 sts; rep from *.

Finishing

Weave in loose ends. Block to finished measurements.

Embellishment

Add assorted buttons and appliqué flowers as shown in photograph. Secure flowers by sewing a bead into the center of each. Use assorted colors to embroider lazy daisies and duplicate-stitch hearts (see page 31 for embroidery instructions) according to the Alphabet chart on page 38. Alternatively, you could embroider family initials or names using the alphabet.

FINISHED SIZE
About 6½" (16.5 cm) wide and
57¾" (146.5 cm) long.

YARN
DK weight (#3 Light).

SHOWN HERE: Louisa Harding
Jasmine (48% cotton, 39% bamboo, 10% silk, 3% polyester; 107 yd
[98 m]/50 g): #15 Pure (A), 4 balls;
#13 Slate (B), 1 ball.

NEEDLES
Body: size U.S. 6 (4 mm).

Edging: size U.S. 3 (3.25 mm).

*Adjust needle size if necessary to
obtain the correct gauge.*

NOTIONS
Beading needle; 860 size 6° pewter
glass beads for scarf; 290 size 6°
lilac silver-lined glass beads for
flowers; stitch holder; tapestry
needle.

GAUGE
22 stitches and 26 rows = 4"
(10 cm) according to Beaded Lace
chart on larger needles.

Nina

Although it looks complicated, this scarf is very simple to
knit—the excitement is in the beads. The scarf is knitted in two
halves so that the leaf-shaped lace pattern has the same ori-
entation on each half to frame the face nicely. Pretty flounces
at the edges add a pleasing feminine silhouette. The contrasting knitted flowers, worked with a delicate beaded cast-on, are
sewn in place after the knitting is complete.

Stitch Guide

Bead 1

On RS rows: With RS facing, bring yarn to front (RS of work), slide a bead next to the st just worked, sl 1 pwise, bring yarn to back (WS of work), leaving bead in front of slipped st. The bead will be secured when the next st is knitted.

On WS rows: With WS facing, bring yarn to back (RS of work), slide a bead next to the st just worked, sl 1 pwise, bring yarn to front (WS of work), leaving bead in front of slipped st. The bead will be secured when the next st is knitted.

Notes

Before beginning, thread the knitting yarn on a beading needle, then thread the desired number of beads onto the yarn.

Each pattern repeat uses 72 beads. Thread enough beads for two or three pattern repeats so that the yarn can move freely through the beads. At the end of the two or three repeats, cut the yarn and thread enough beads for two or three more repeats. Weave in the loose ends when finishing the scarf.

Scarf Half (make 2)

Flounce

Thread 70 beads pewter glass beads for edging flounce.

With A and smaller needles, CO 109 sts. Work 3 rows in garter st (knit every row), ending with a RS row.

BEAD ROW 1: (WS) K1, [*p1, bead 1 (see Stitch Guide)] 53 times, p1, k1.

Work 2 rows in garter st, ending with a WS row. Change to larger needles and work 10 rows even in St st (knit RS rows; purl WS rows), ending with a WS row.

DEC ROW 1: (RS) *Sl 1, k2tog, psso; rep from * to last st, k1—37 sts rem.

Work 2 rows even in garter st.

BEAD ROW 2: (WS) K1, *p1, bead 1; rep from * to last 2 sts, p1, k1.

DEC ROW 2: K35, k2tog—36 sts rem.

Knit 1 row even—piece measures 2¾" (7 cm) from CO.

Body

Cut yarn and thread enough beads for 2 or 3 pattern reps (see Notes). Work Rows 1–32 of Beaded Lace chart 5 times, threading additional beads on yarn as necessary—piece measures about 27¼" (69 cm) from CO. Place sts on holder.

Make another piece to match.

BEADED LACE CHART

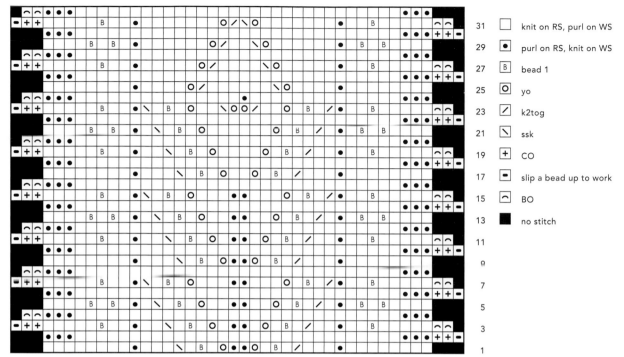

31	☐	knit on RS, purl on WS
29	●	purl on RS, knit on WS
27	B	bead 1
25	O	yo
23	/	k2tog
21	⊼	ssk
19	+	CO
17	▬	slip a bead up to work
15	⌒	BO
13	◼	no stitch

Finishing

Weave in loose ends. Block to finished measurements.

Place 36 sts of each half onto separate needles. With RS tog, use the three-needle method (see Glossary) to BO all sts tog.

Beaded Flower (make 10)

Thread 29 lilac silver-lined beads onto B (see Notes). With smaller needles and using the long-tail method (see Glossary), work beaded CO as foll: make a slipknot on needle, slide a bead up to work, CO 1 st (2 sts on needle), *slide a bead up to work, CO 1 st; rep from * until all 29 beads have been used—30 sts total.

ROW 1: K1, BO 3 sts (2 sts on right-hand needle), *k1, BO 3 sts; rep from * 4 more times—12 sts rem.

Cut yarn, thread tail through rem sts, pull tight to close hole, and secure with a few sts.

With yarn threaded on a tapestry needle, sew beaded flowers onto each rep of Row 23, centered over the double yo and leaving the eyelet hole open for flower center.

FINISHED SIZE
About 10¾" (27.5 cm) wide, 13¼"
(33.5 cm) long, and 4" (10 cm)
deep.

YARN
Chunky weight (#5 Bulky).

SHOWN HERE: Louisa Harding
Millais (50% wool, 50% acrylic;
65 yd [60 m]/50 g): #6 Blackcur-
rant (purple; A) and #10 Grey (D),
2 balls each; #4 Pottage (green;
B) and #2 Cottage Rose (C), 1 ball
each.

NEEDLES
Body: size U.S. 10½ (7 mm).

Edging: size U.S. 10 (6 mm).

*Adjust needle size if necessary to
obtain the correct gauge.*

NOTIONS
One set of 8" (20.5 cm) round-top
bamboo bag handles; piece of felt
for lining measuring 12" (30.5 cm)
wide and 24" (61 cm) long; piece
of iron-on heavyweight interfacing
measuring 12" (30.5 cm) wide and
24" (61 cm) long; piece of card
stock or stiff paper measuring 4"
(10 cm) wide and 10½" (26.5 cm)
long; nine assorted gray pearl buttons; assorted lengths of 2" (5 cm)
and ¼" (6 mm) ribbons; one 1½"
(3.8 cm) vintage belt buckle.

GAUGE
13 stitches and 20 rows = 4"
(10 cm) in seed stitch on larger
needles.

Ivy

Worked in seed stitch with bulky yarn, this purse knits up in a
few short hours. It's the time spent embellishing afterward that
transforms it into a something wonderful. I added knitted flowers, pom-poms, ribbons, and buttons for a riotous look. Have
fun with this project, but pin the embellishments in place to
make sure you have haven't gone over the top—in some cases,
less is more.

First Half

With A and smaller needles, CO 49 sts. Work 2 rows in garter st (knit every row). *Change to B and larger needles. Work seed-st patt as foll:

ROW 1: (RS) [K1, p1] 3 times, k3, [p1, k1] 15 times, p1, k3, [p1, k1] 3 times.

ROW 2: *K1, p1; rep from * to last st, k1.

Keeping in patt as established, work the foll color sequence: 2 rows C, 2 rows A, 2 rows D, 2 rows C, 2 rows D.

With D, work eyelet band as foll:

ROWS 1, 3, AND 5: (RS) P7, k1, p33, k1, p7.

ROW 2: Purl.

ROW 4: K2, [yo, p2tog] 2 times, k1, p1, k2, [yo, p2tog] 15 times, k1, p1, k2, [yo, p2tog] 2 times, k1.

ROW 6: Purl.

Cont in seed-st patt as before and work the foll color sequence: 2 rows D, 2 rows B, 2 rows D, 2 rows C, 2 rows B, 4 rows D, 2 rows C, 2 rows D, 2 rows C, 2 rows A, 4 rows D, 2 rows A, 2 rows B, 2 rows D, 2 rows B, 2 rows C, 2 rows A, 2 rows B, 4 rows A.

With A and cont in seed-st patt, BO 7 sts at beg of next 2 rows—35 sts rem.

Base

Purl 1 RS row for fold line.

NEXT ROW: (WS) *K1, p1; rep from * to last st, k1.

NEXT ROW: *K1, p1; rep from * to last st, k1.

Rep the last 2 rows 8 more times, ending with a RS row—piece measures about 17" (43 cm) from CO. Knit 1 WS row for fold line.

Second Half

Cont in seed-st patt, use the cable method (see Glossary) to CO 7 sts at beg of next 2 rows—49 sts. Cont in patt, work the foll color sequence: 4 rows A, 2 rows B, 2 rows A, 2 rows C, 2 rows B, 2 rows D, 2 rows B, 2 rows A, 4 rows D, 2 rows A, 2 rows C, 2 rows D, 2 rows C, 4 rows D, 2 rows B, 2 rows C, 2 rows D, 2 rows B, 2 rows D.

With D, work 6-row eyelet band as before. Cont in seed-st patt, work the foll color sequence: 2 rows D, 2 rows C, 2 rows D, 2 rows A, 2 rows C, 2 rows B, 1 row A.

Change to smaller needles and work 2 rows in garter st. With WS facing, BO all sts knitwise.

Handle Gussets

With A, smaller needles, RS facing, and beg 12 sts in from right side edge, pick up and knit 25 sts. Knit 1 WS row. Work 4 rows even in St st (knit RS rows; purl WS rows). Purl 1 RS row to form turning ridge. Work 4 more rows in St st. BO all sts. Rep for other end of purse.

Finishing

Weave in loose ends. Block to finished measurements.

Flowers *(make 9)*

With oddments of yarn and smaller needles, CO 30 sts.

ROW 1: *K1, BO 3 sts (2 sts on right-hand needle); rep from * to end—12 sts rem.

Cut yarn leaving a 10" (25.5 cm) tail. Thread tail through rem sts, pull to make a ⅜" (1 cm) hole in center, and secure with a few sts. With yarn threaded on a tapestry needle, sew flowers to RS of purse, attaching a button in the center of each flower.

pom-pom

Cut two circles of cardboard, each ½"
(1.3 cm) larger than desired finished
pom-pom width. Cut a small circle out
of the center and a small wedge out of
the side of each circle (Figure 1). Tie a
strand of yarn between the circle, hold
circles together and wrap with yarn—the
more wraps, the denser the pom-pom.
Cut between the circles and knot the tie
strand tightly (Figure 2). Place pom-pom
between two smaller cardboard circles
held together with a needle and trim
the edges (Figure 3).

FIGURE 1

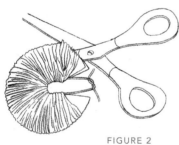

FIGURE 2

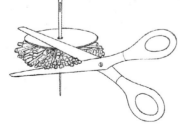

FIGURE 3

Assembly

Using purse as a template, cut out lining fabric and interfacing fabric. Place interfacing on WS of purse body and iron in place according to manufacturer's directions. Trim side edges as necessary. With WS tog, fold knitted piece along bottom fold lines. With yarn threaded on a tapestry needle, use a mattress st (see Glossary) to sew side seams.

Turn purse inside out and use backstitches (see Glossary) to sew side gusset seam (BO/CO sts to the selvedge edges of the base to create a flat base).

Using a large needle, poke a hole in each corner of the card stock. Place card stock in base of purse and with sharp-point sewing needle and matching thread, secure in place through the holes.

Turn purse right side out. Sew purse handles in place.

Lining

With WS facing and using a backstitch with a ⅜" (1 cm) seam allowance, sew side seams. Use a backstitch to sew gusset seams as for purse. With WS tog, place lining inside knitted bag, fold over ¾" (2 cm) at top, and whipstitch (see Glossary) in place just below CO/BO edge.

Other Embellishments

Thread a ¼" (6 mm) ribbon through the eyelet band. Thread 2" ribbon through vintage belt buckle and tie into a big bow. Secure with a few sts and attach to purse as desired.

More Extras

For extra embellishment, make two 2" (5 cm) pom-poms (see page 115), one with A and one with D. Make 2 knitted chains (one with A and one with D) as foll:

Begin with a sl st on larger needle, k1, slip st from right-hand needle to left-hand needle; rep from * until piece measures about 10" (25.5 cm). Fasten off.

Attach pom-poms to chains of like color, then secure chains to bamboo handles. If desired, thread a purchased flower corsage through the belt buckle and secure with a few sts.

April

Knitted flowers and buttons embellish this quick and simple—and très chic—bolero. For both versions, I knitted the flowers with bits of Grace Silk and Wool in soft dusky pastel shades, then attached them to the left front with complementary buttons. The blossom-shaped buttons come from a fabulous Parisian store called La Droguerie; check out thrift stores for vintage buttons in your area. A satin ribbon tied with a generous bow adds feminine grace.

Hulda version.

Back

With larger needles, CO 51 (55, 59, 63, 67, 71) sts. Beg with a RS row, work 6 rows in St st (knit RS rows; purl WS rows).

INC ROW: (RS) K3, M1 (see Glossary), knit to last 3 sts, M1, k3—2 sts inc'd.

Work 5 rows even in St st. Rep the last 6 rows 3 more times—59 (63, 67, 71, 75, 79) sts. Work even until piece measures 8" (20.5 cm) from CO, ending with a WS row.

Shape Armholes

BO 3 (4, 4, 5, 5, 6) sts at beg of next 2 rows, then BO 2 (2, 3, 3, 3, 3) sts at beg of foll 2 rows—49 (51, 53, 55, 59, 61) sts rem.

DEC ROW: (RS) K3, k2tog, knit to last 5 sts, ssk, k3—2 sts dec'd.

Purl 1 WS row. Rep the last 2 rows 1 (1, 2, 2, 3, 3) more times—45 (47, 47, 49, 51, 53) sts rem. Work even until armholes measure 7 (7, 7½, 7½, 8, 8)" (18 [18, 19, 19, 20.5, 20.5] cm), ending with a WS row.

Shape Shoulders

Right Shoulder

BO 4 (4, 4, 4, 5, 5) sts at beg of next 2 rows—37 (39, 39, 41, 41, 43) sts rem.

NEXT ROW: (RS) BO 4 (4, 4, 4, 5, 5) sts, knit until there are 6 (7, 7, 8, 7, 8) sts on right-hand needle, turn work—6 (7, 7, 8, 7, 8) right shoulder sts; rem 27 (28, 28, 29, 29, 30) sts will be worked later for neck and left shoulder. With WS facing, BO 3 sts, purl to end—3 (4, 4, 5, 4, 5) sts rem. BO rem sts.

Left Shoulder

With RS facing, keep center 17 sts on holder, rejoin yarn to held sts, BO center 17 sts, knit to end—10 (11, 11, 12, 12, 13) sts rem. With WS facing, BO 4 (4, 4, 4, 5, 5) sts, purl to end—6 (7, 7, 8, 7, 8) sts rem. With RS facing, BO 3 sts, knit to end—3 (4, 4, 5, 4, 5) sts rem. BO rem sts.

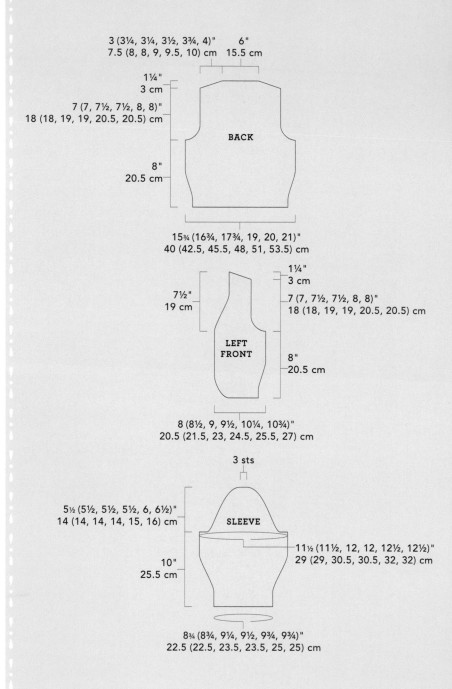

Left Front

With larger needles, CO 23 (25, 27, 29, 31, 33) sts. Beg with a RS row, work 2 rows in St st.

INC ROW 1: (RS) Knit to last 3 sts, M1, k3—1 st inc'd.

Work 1 WS row even. Rep the last 2 rows once more—25 (27, 29, 31, 33, 35) sts.

INC ROW 2: (RS) K3, M1, knit to last 3 sts, M1, k3—27 (29, 31, 33, 35, 37) sts.

Work 5 rows even in St st.

INC ROW 3: (RS) K3, M1, knit to end—1 st inc'd.

Work 5 rows even in St st. Rep the last 6 rows 2 more times—30 (32, 34, 36, 38, 40) sts. Work even until piece measures 8" (20.5 cm) from CO, ending with a WS row.

Shape Armhole and Neck

At armhole edge (beg of RS rows), BO 3 (4, 4, 5, 5, 6) sts once, then BO 2 (2, 3, 3, 3, 3) sts once—25 (26, 27, 28, 30, 31) sts rem. Work 1 WS row even.

DEC ROW 1: (RS) K3, k2tog, knit to last 5 sts, ssk, k3—2 sts dec'd.

Work 1 WS row even. Rep the last 2 rows 1 (1, 2, 2, 3, 3) more time(s)—21 (22, 21, 22, 22, 23) sts rem. Purl 1 WS row.

DEC ROW 2: (RS) Knit to last 5 sts, ssk, k3—1 st dec'd.

Rep the last 2 rows 9 (9, 8, 8, 7, 7) more times—11 (12, 12, 13, 14, 15) sts rem. Work even until armhole measures 7 (7, 7½, 7½, 8, 8)" (18 [18, 19, 19, 20.5, 20.5] cm), ending with a WS row.

Shape Shoulder

At armhole edge, BO 4 (4, 4, 4, 5, 5) sts 2 times, then BO rem 3 (4, 5, 4, 5) sts.

Right Front

With larger needles, CO 23 (25, 27, 29, 31, 33) sts. Beg with a RS row, work 2 rows in St st.

INC ROW 1: (RS) K3, M1, knit to end—1 st inc'd.

Work 1 WS row even. Rep the last 2 rows once more—25 (27, 29, 31, 33, 35) sts.

INC ROW 2: (RS) K3, M1, knit to last 3 sts, M1, k3—27 (29, 31, 33, 35, 37) sts.

Work 5 rows even in St st.

INC ROW 3: (RS) Knit to last 3 sts, M1, k3—1 st inc'd.

Work 5 rows even in St st. Rep the last 6 rows 2 more times—30 (32, 34, 36, 38, 40) sts. Work even until piece measures 8" (20.5 cm) from CO, ending with a RS row.

Shape Armhole and Neck

At armhole edge (beg of WS rows), BO 3 (4, 4, 5, 5, 6) sts once, then BO 2 (2, 3, 3, 3, 3) sts once—25 (26, 27, 28, 30, 31) sts rem.

DEC ROW 1: (RS) K3, k2tog, knit to last 5 sts, ssk, k3—2 sts dec'd.

Work 1 WS row even. Rep the last 2 rows 1 (1, 2, 2, 3, 3) more time(s)—21 (22, 21, 22, 22, 23) sts rem. Purl 1 WS row.

DEC ROW 2: (RS) K3, k2tog, knit to end—1 st dec'd.

Rep the last 2 rows 9 (9, 8, 8, 7, 7) more times—11 (12, 12, 13, 14, 15) sts rem. Work even until armhole measures 7 (7, 7½, 7½, 8, 8)" (18 [18, 19, 19, 20.5, 20.5] cm), ending with a RS row.

Shape Shoulder

At armhole edge, BO 4 (4, 4, 4, 5, 5) sts 2 times, then BO rem 3 (4, 4, 5, 4, 5) sts.

Sleeves

With smaller needles, work the picot CO as folls: *Use the cable method (see Glossary) to CO 5 sts, BO 2 sts, sl st on right-hand needle back onto left-hand needle; rep from * until there are 33 (33, 33, 33, 36, 36) sts, use the cable method to CO 0 (0, 2, 2, 1, 1) more st(s)—33 (33, 35, 35, 37, 37) sts. Work 4 rows in garter st. Change to larger needles. Beg with a RS row, work 6 rows in St st.

INC ROW: (RS) K3, M1, knit to last 3 sts, M1, k3—2 sts inc'd.

Work 5 rows even in St st. Rep the last 6 rows 4 more times—43 (43, 45, 45, 47, 47) sts. Work even until piece measures 10" (25.5 cm) from CO, ending with a WS row.

Shape Cap

BO 3 (4, 4, 5, 5, 6) sts at beg of next 2 rows—37 (35, 37, 35, 37, 35) sts rem.

DEC ROW 1: (RS) Ssk, knit to last 2 sts, k2tog—2 sts dec'd.

DEC ROW 2: (WS) P2tog, purl to last 2 sts, ssp (see Glossary)—2 sts dec'd.

Rep Dec Row 1 once more, then every other row 2 more times, then every 4th row 3 (3, 3, 3, 3, 4) times, then every other row 1 (1, 1, 1, 2, 1) time(s)—19 (17, 19, 17, 17, 15) sts rem.

NEXT ROW: (WS) Rep Dec Row 2—2 sts dec'd.

NEXT ROW: (RS) Rep Dec Row 1—2 sts dec'd.

NEXT ROW: (WS) Rep Dec Row 2—13 (11, 13, 11, 11, 9) sts rem.

BO 3 sts at beg of next 2 rows—7 (5, 7, 5, 5, 3) sts rem. BO all sts.

Finishing

Block pieces to finished measurements. With yarn threaded on a tapestry needle, use a mattress st (see Glossary) to sew fronts to back at shoulders. Sew left side seam in the same way. Weave in loose ends.

Lower Edging

With smaller needles, RS facing, and beg at right side seam, pick up and knit 23 (25, 27, 29, 31, 33) sts along right front CO edge, 6 sts around curve, 25 sts along right front edge to start of neck shaping, 27 (27, 29, 29, 31, 31) sts along right front neck edge to shoulder, 3 sts in BO neck sts, k17 held back neck sts, pick up and knit 3 sts in BO neck sts, 27 (27, 29, 29, 31, 31) sts along left front neck to end of neck shaping, 25 sts along left front edge, 6 sts around curve, 23 (25, 27, 29, 31, 33) sts along left front CO edge, and 51 (55, 59, 63, 67, 71) sts across back CO edge—236 (244, 256, 264, 276, 284) sts total. Knit 1 WS row.

INC ROW: (RS) K24 (26, 28, 30, 32, 34), M1, [k2, M1] 2 times, k128 (128, 132, 132, 136, 136), [M1, k2] 2 times, M1, knit to end—242 (250, 262, 270, 282, 290) sts.

Knit 2 rows. With WS facing, work picot BO as foll: BO 5 (4, 4, 3, 3, 5) sts, *sl st on right-hand needle back onto left-hand needle, use the cable method to CO 2 sts, BO 5 sts; rep from * to end.

Seams

With yarn threaded on a tapestry needle, use a mattress st to sew right side seam. Sew sleeve seams. Sew sleeve caps into armholes, matching centers of BO edges to shoulder seams and easing to fit into armholes.

Ribbon Ties

Cut ribbon in two equal lengths. Measure 4" (10 cm) up from CO edge of right front. With sewing thread and sharp-point sewing needle, make a small turn-back seam in ribbon, then sew to WS of right front with small whipstitches (see Glossary). Rep for left front.

Flowers (*make 14*)

With appropriate size needles to match the oddments of yarn, CO 36 sts.

ROW 1: *K1, BO 4 sts (2 sts on needle); rep from * to end—12 sts rem.

Thread yarn through rem sts, pull tight, and secure into flower shape with a few stitches.

Pin the flowers randomly on left front and sew in place with yarn. Sew a flower-shaped button to center of each knitted flower. Attach other flower-shaped buttons as desired.

Rosetti version.

FINISHED SIZE
About 8½" (21.5 cm) wide and 10"
(25.5 cm) long.

YARN
Chunky weight (#5 Bulky).

SHOWN HERE: Louisa Harding
Millais (50% wool, 50% acrylic;
65 yd [60 m]/50 g): #2 Cottage
Rose, 2 balls.

NEEDLES
Body: size U.S. 10½ (7 mm).

Flounce and eyelet band: size U.S.
10 (6 mm).

*Adjust needle size if necessary to
obtain the correct gauge.*

NOTIONS
31 assorted charms or beads;
stitch holder; 79"(2 m) of ⅝"
(1.5 cm) ribbon; 48 size 6° pewter
glass beads; eighteen ½" (1.3 cm)
flower-shaped sequins, piece of
felt measuring 9" (23 cm) wide and
20" (51 cm) long for lining; sharp-
point sewing needle and matching
thread.

GAUGE
13 stitches and 15 rows = 4"
(10 cm) in lace pattern on larger
needles.

Marigold

I sometimes feel a deep connection to my grandmother and
the women of her generation, the original recyclers. They never
threw anything away that could be reused or reworked. In hom-
age to that practice, this purse includes charms from a broken
charm bracelet that has been waiting for a flash of inspiration. I
worked the charms into the picot edging at the top of the purse.
I enjoy carrying the sentiment of my bracelet in a new guise.

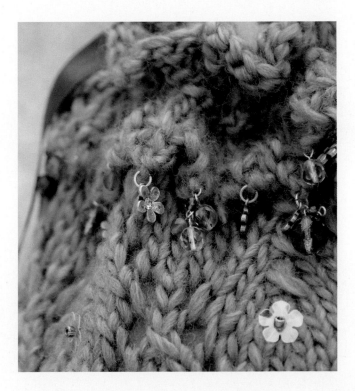

Notes

Although I used charms, you can substitute beads in different shapes, sizes, and colors.

If the holes in the charms or beads are too small, thread a fine wire through the beads, twist the wire into a loop, and thread the yarn through the wire loop.

Purse

Flounce

Thread 31 beads or charms onto yarn. With smaller needles, work beaded picot CO as foll: Use the cable method (see Glossary) to CO 4 sts, *slide a charm or bead up to work, BO 2 sts, sl st on right-hand needle onto left-hand needle (2 sts on left-hand needle); rep from * 30 more times (62 sts on needle), use the cable method to CO 1 st—63 sts total.

Beg with a RS row, work 2 rows in St st (knit RS rows; purl WS rows). Place sts on holder. Cut yarn.

Body

With larger needles, CO 63 sts. Beg with a RS row, work 2 rows in St st. Work Rows 1–16 of Lace chart 2 times. Beg with a RS row, work 2 rows in St st, ending with a WS row.

Join Flounce

Place 63 held flounce sts on spare needle and hold WS of flounce in front of RS of body. With smaller needles, join the pieces by knitting the sts on the two needles tog as if to k2tog—63 sts.

LACE CHART

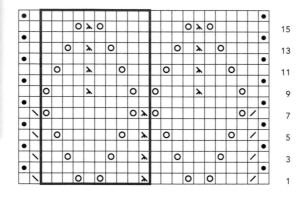

☐ knit on RS, purl on WS

▣ purl on RS, knit on WS

◢ k2tog

◣ ssk

⅄ sl 1, k2tog, psso

⊙ yo

◻ pattern repeat

Eyelet Band

Work 2 rows in garter st (knit every row).

EYELET ROW: (WS) K1, p1, *yo, p2tog; rep from * to last st, k1.

Work 3 rows in garter st, ending with a RS row. With WS facing, BO all sts knitwise.

Finishing

Weave in loose ends. Block to finished measurements.

Assembly

With yarn threaded on a tapestry needle, use a mattress st (see Glossary) to sew side seams, working the selvedge st in the seam allowance. Fold piece in half with seam at center back. With RS facing, use a whipstitch (see Glossary) to sew lower edge of bag (CO edge) closed.

Embellishments

With sharp-point sewing needle and matching thread, sew a charm or bead to each CO st at lower edge of purse.

Sew a flower sequin to the center of each lace motif, adding a pewter bead in the center of each.

Cut ribbon in half. Beg at opposite sides of the purse, thread each length in and out of the eyelet holes at the top of the purse. Knot the ends.

Lining

Fold felted lining fabric in half at bottom edge. Use a backstitch (see Glossary) with a ⅜" (1 cm) seam allowance to sew side seams. Slip bag lining inside purse, turn a ⅜" (1 cm) seam at top, and use a whipstitch to secure just below eyelet band.

GLOSSARY

Abbreviations

beg	begin(s); beginning	p	purl	st	stitch(es)
BO	bind off	p1f&b	purl into front and back of same stitch	St st	stockinette stitch
CC	contrast color			tbl	through back loop
cm	centimeter(s)	patt(s)	pattern(s)	tog	together
cn	cable needle	psso	pass slipped stitch over	WS	wrong side
CO	cast on	pwise	purlwise, as if to purl	wyb	with yarn in back
cont	continue(s); continuing	rem	remain(s); remaining	wyf	with yarn in front
dec(s)	decrease(s); decreasing	rep	repeat(s); repeating	yd	yard(s)
dpn	double-pointed needles	rev St st	reverse stockinette stitch	yo	yarnover
foll	follow(s); following	rnd(s)	round(s)	*	repeat starting point
g	gram(s)	RS	right side	* *	repeat all instructions between asterisks
inc(s)	increase(s); increasing	sl	slip		
k	knit	sl st	slip st (slip 1 stitch purlwise unless otherwise indicated)	( )	alternate measurements and/ or instructions
k1f&b	knit into the front and back of same stitch				
kwise	knitwise, as if to knit	ssk	slip 2 stitches knitwise, one at a time, from the left needle to right needle, insert left needle tip through both front loops and knit together from this position (1 stitch decrease)	[ ]	work instructions as a group a specified number of times
m	marker(s)				
MC	main color				
mm	millimeter(s)				
M1	make one (increase)				

Bind-Offs

Three-Needle Bind-Off

Place the stitches to be joined onto two separate needles and hold the needles parallel so that the right sides of knitting face together. Insert a third needle into the first stitch on each of two needles (Figure 1) and knit them together as one stitch (Figure 2), *knit the next stitch on each needle the same way, then use the left needle tip to lift the first stitch over the second and off the needle (Figure 3). Repeat from * until no stitches remain on first two needles. Cut yarn and pull tail through last stitch to secure.

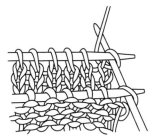

FIGURE 1

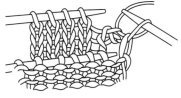

FIGURE 2

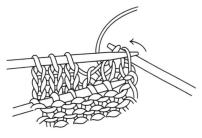

FIGURE 3

Cast-Ons

Backward-Loop Cast-On

*Loop working yarn and place it on needle backward so that it doesn't unwind. Repeat from *.

Cable Cast-On

If there are no stitches on the needles, make a slipknot of working yarn and place it on the needle, then use the knitted method to cast-on one more stitch—two stitches on needle. Hold needle with working yarn in your left hand with the wrong side of the work facing you. *Insert right needle between the first two stitches on left needle (Figure 1), wrap yarn around needle as if to knit, draw yarn through (Figure 2), and place new loop on left needle (Figure 3) to form a new stitch. Repeat from * for the desired number of stitches, always working between the first two stitches on the left needle.

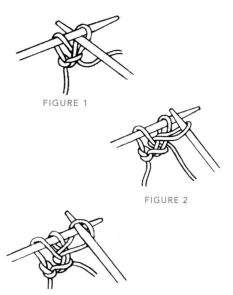

FIGURE 1

FIGURE 2

FIGURE 3

Long-Tail (Continental) Cast-On

Leaving a long tail (about ½" [1.3 cm] for each stitch to be cast on), make a slipknot and place on right needle. Place thumb and index finger of your left hand between the yarn ends so that working yarn is around your index finger and tail end is around your thumb and secure the yarn ends with your other fingers. Hold your palm upward, making a V of yarn (Figure 1). *Bring needle up through loop on thumb (Figure 2), catch first strand around index finger, and go back down through loop on thumb (Figure 3). Drop loop off thumb and, placing thumb back in V configuration, tighten resulting stitch on needle (Figure 4). Repeat from * for the desired number of stitches.

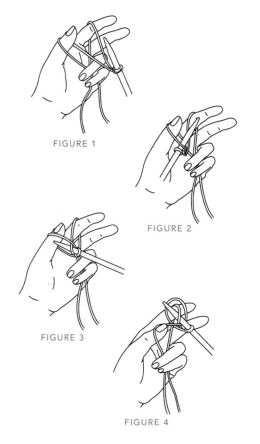

FIGURE 1

FIGURE 2

FIGURE 3

FIGURE 4

Decreases

Knit 2 Together Through Back Loops (k2togtbl)

Insert right needle through the back loops of the next two stitches on the left needle from front to back), wrap the yarn around the needle, and pull a loop through while slipping the stitches off the left needle.

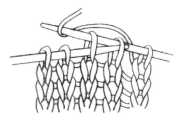

Slip, Slip, Purl (ssp)

Holding yarn in front, slip two stitches individually knitwise (Figure 1), then slip these two stitches back onto left needle (they will be twisted on the needle) and purl them together through their back loops (Figure 2).

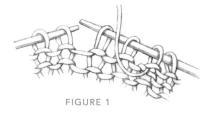

FIGURE 1

FIGURE 2

Increases

Knit in the Front and Back (k1f&b)

Knit into a stitch but leave it on the left needle (Figure 1), then knit through the back loop of the same stitch (Figure 2) and slip the original stitch off the needle (Figure 3).

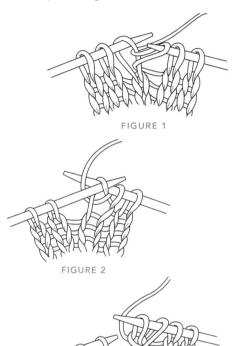

FIGURE 1

FIGURE 2

FIGURE 3

Make One (M1)

Note: Use the left slant if no direction of slant is specified.

Left Slant (M1L)

With left needle tip, lift the strand between the last knitted stitch and the first stitch on the left needle from front to back (Figure 1), then knit the lifted loop through the back (Figure 2).

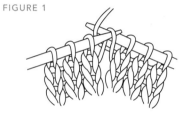

FIGURE 1

FIGURE 2

Right Slant (M1R)

With left needle tip, lift the strand between the needles from back to front (Figure 1), then knit the lifted loop through the front (Figure 2).

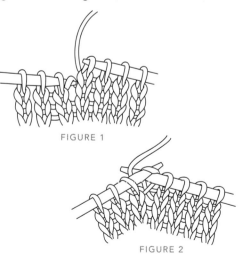

FIGURE 1

FIGURE 2

Seams

Backstitch

Pin pieces to be seamed with right sides facing together. Working from right to left into the edge stitch, bring threaded needle up between the next two stitches on each piece of knitted fabric, then back down through both layers, one stitch to the right of the starting point (Figure 1). *Bring the needle up through both layers a stitch to the left of the backstitch just made (Figure 2), then back down to the right, through the same hole used before (Figure 3). Repeat from *, working backward one stitch for every two stitches worked forward.

Mattress Stitch

Place the pieces to be seamed on a table, right sides facing up. Begin at the lower edge and work upward as follows for your stitch pattern:

Stockinette Stitch with 1-Stitch Seam Allowance

Insert threaded needle under one bar between the two edge stitches on one piece, then under the corresponding bar plus the bar above it on the other piece (Figure 1). *Pick up the next two bars on the first piece (Figure 2), then the next two bars on the other (Figure 3). Repeat from *, ending by picking up the last bar or pair of bars on the first piece.

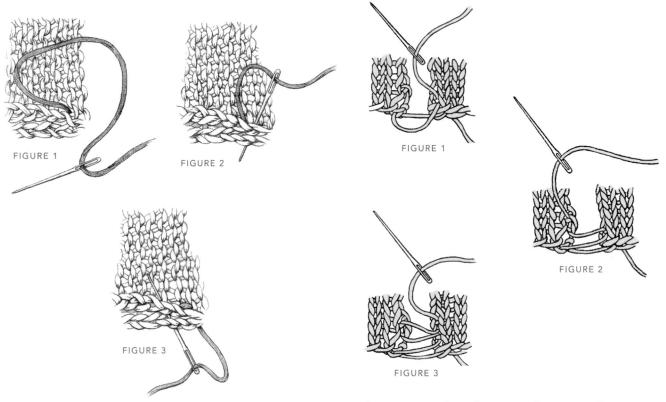

FIGURE 1

FIGURE 2

FIGURE 3

FIGURE 1

FIGURE 2

FIGURE 3

Stockinette Stitch with ½-Stitch Seam Allowance

To reduce bulk in the mattress-stitch seam, work as for the 1-stitch seam allowance but pick up the bars in the center of the edge stitches instead of between the last two stitches.

Whipstitch

Hold pieces to be sewn together so that the edges to be seamed are even with each other. With yarn threaded on a tapestry needle, *insert needle through both layers from back to front, then bring needle to back. Repeat from *, keeping even tension on the seaming yarn.

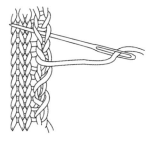

Short-Rows

Short-Rows Knit Side

Work to turning point, slip next stitch purlwise (Figure 1), bring the yarn to the front, then slip the same stitch back to the left needle (Figure 2), turn the work around and bring the yarn in position for the next stitch—one stitch has been wrapped and the yarn is correctly positioned to work the next stitch. When you come to a wrapped stitch on a subsequent row, hide the wrap by working it together with the wrapped stitch as follows: Insert right needle tip under the wrap (from the front if wrapped stitch is a knit stitch; from the back if wrapped stitch is a purl stitch; Figure 3), then into the stitch on the needle, and work the stitch and its wrap together as a single stitch.

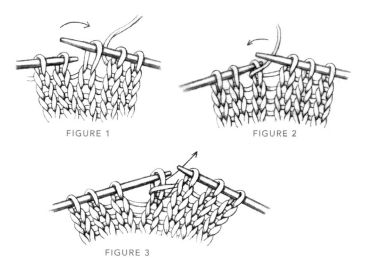

FIGURE 1   FIGURE 2

FIGURE 3

Short-Rows Purl Side

Work to the turning point, slip the next stitch purlwise to the right needle, bring the yarn to the back of the work (Figure 1), return the slipped stitch to the left needle, bring the yarn to the front between the needles (Figure 2), and turn the work so that the knit side is facing—one stitch has been wrapped and the yarn is correctly positioned to knit the next stitch. To hide the wrap on a subsequent purl row, work to the wrapped stitch, use the tip of the right needle to pick up the wrap from the back, place it on the left needle (Figure 3), then purl it together with the wrapped stitch.

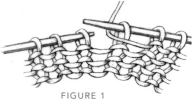

FIGURE 1

FIGURE 2

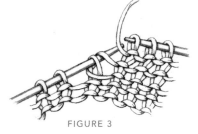

FIGURE 3

Sources for Yarn

The following companies distribute Louisa Harding Yarns. Visit their websites for helpful information regarding yarns, shade cards, and yarn store locations.

Australia
Prestige Yarns
prestigeyarns.com
+61 02 4285 6669

Canada
Diamond Yarn
diamondyarn.com
(416) 736-6111

Europe
Designer Yarns
designeryarns.uk.com
+44 (0) 1535 664222

United States
Knitting Fever Inc.
knittingfever.com
(516) 546-3600

Substituting Yarns

For each project in this book, yarn choice is an inherent factor in the overall design. If you want to substitute a different yarn, be sure to choose a yarn (and needles) that has a similar weight and that produces exactly the same gauge specified in the instructions. If your gauge is different, the project will turn out a different size, something that can be disastrous in a garment. Always knit a swatch to test the gauge before embarking on a project. That said, it can be fun to substitute yarns for different looks and effects, and the process can get you thinking creatively about your knitting.

Sources for Embellishments

The following companies and stores are at the top of my list when I'm looking for embellishment extras. They sell all the ribbons, bows, buttons, beads, buckles, and feathers that a creative magpie desires. Many yarn stores sell similar items (because most are run by creative magpies).

La Droguerie à Paris
9 et 11 rue de jour
75001 Paris
ladroguerie.com
Exquisite buttons, closures, pressed velvet applique flowers, feathers, purse handles, jacquard, velvet and satin ribbons, and so much more.

VV Rouleaux
102 Marylebone Ln.
London W1U 2QD
vvrouleaux.com
Beautiful ribbons, feathers and trimmings.

Debbie Abrahams Beads
debbieabrahams.com
A wonderful selection of beads specifically selected for knitting with.

Button Shoppe
buttonshoppe.com
Unusual buttons and closures.

M & J Trimming
mjtrim.com
Ribbons of all kinds, buttons, buckles, and more.

Purl Soho
purlsoho.com
Jumbo rickrack, Japanese twill tapes, silk embroidery floss, unusual ribbons (and yarn, too!).

Vintage Vogue
vintagevogue.com
Mokuba ribbons and ribbon flowers, wool felt, charms, chenille thread, and more.

INDEX

Find even more *inspiring detailed knitting designs* with these beautiful resources from Interweave

Feminine Knits
22 Timeless Designs
Lene Holme Samsøe
ISBN 978-1-59668-140-8
$22.95

French Girl Knits
*Innovative Techniques,
Romantic Details, and
Feminine Designs*
Kristeen Griffin-Grimes
ISBN 978-1-59668-069-2
$24.95

Knitting Little Luxuries
*Beautiful Accessories
to Knit*
Louisa Harding
ISBN 978-1-59668-054-8
$21.95

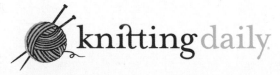

Join KnittingDaily.com, an online community that shares your passion for knitting. You'll get a free e-newsletter, free patterns, projects store, a daily blog, even updates, galleries, tips and techniques, and more. Sign up for *Knitting Daily* at **knittingdaily.com**.

From cover to cover, *Interweave Knits* magazine presents great projects for the beginner to the advanced knitter. Every issue is packed full of captivating smart designs, step-by-step instructions, easy-to-understand illustrations, plus well-written, lively articles sure to inspire. **Interweaveknits.com**

INTERWEAVE
interweave.com